vital
vegetables

vital
vegetables

Over 200 original recipes and ideas from *BBC Good Food* and *BBC Vegetarian Good Food* magazines

Published by BBC Worldwide Ltd,
Woodlands, 80 Wood Lane,
London W12 OTT

Designed and produced by
Quadrille Publishing Limited,
Alhambra House,
27–31 Charing Cross Road,
London WC2H OLS

First published 1999
Text © The contributors 1999
Photography © The photographers 1999
(For a full list of contributors and
photographers see page 156.)
Original material, design & layout © 1999
Quadrille Publishing Limited

ISBN 0 563 55109 7

Editor & Project Manager: Lewis Esson
Editorial Director: Jane O'Shea
Art Director: Mary Evans
Design: Paul Welti and Coralie Bickford-Smith
Editorial Assistant: Caroline Perkins
Project Editor for the BBC: Vicki Vrint
Production: Julie Hadingham

Printed and bound in Singapore by
KHL Printing Co Pte Ltd
Colour separations by Colourscan, Singapore

Throughout the book recipes are for four
people unless otherwise stated. Both metric
and imperial quantities are given. Use either
all metric or all imperial, as the two are not
necessarily interchangeable.

contents

introduction

Vegetables have undergone a radical repositioning in our cooking over the last decade – from being the stalwart reliable background fillers in our meals to all-singing, all-dancing leading roles in all courses.

Of course, vegetarians have been giving them star billing for some time now, and their influence – combined with the influence of Mediterranean, especially Italian, cuisine on our culture – has spread so widely that there is now an almost universal acceptance that meals no longer need to consist of 'meat and two veg'. Exciting and tasty vegetable dishes are also enjoyed these days by everyone, without their necessarily even realizing that the food they are relishing so much is actually meat-free.

In this lavish new cookbook, compiled from *BBC Good Food* and *BBC Vegetarian Good Food* magazines, you will find over 200 original recipes and ideas for a vast range of mouthwatering ways with vegetables – some so simple they can be made in a matter of minutes for a quick snack, starter or appealing side dish; others so spectacular or inspired they are guaranteed to have friends or family sitting up and taking notice. There are dishes for all occasions, budget levels and all seasons – including many that can be made entirely, or in part, ahead of time.

Every recipe has been tried and tested by the *BBC Good Food* and *BBC Vegetarian Good Food* teams in the magazines' test kitchens and a wealth of splendid photographs shows quite how good vegetable dishes can look. Most chapters include at least one feature on a particular vegetable – either an old favourite, such as the potato, or a relative unknown like the Jerusalem artichoke – crammed with information on how to choose, store and prepare the vegetables so that you can buy and cook them with more confidence.

Because everything is explained with such care and expertise, in the magazines' characteristic clear and user-friendly way, it makes no difference whether you are a beginner or an experienced cook, this book should be on every kitchen shelf.

Among the most comforting of dishes are soups made from masses of tasty vegetables, be they nourishing clear broths or thick hearty purées. At their heart usually lies a good flavoursome stock, which may also form the basis for many classic sauces. Soups also provide an opportunity to try new combinations of vegetables, flavourings and spices.

Taking Stock

Soups, Stocks and Sauces

Spicy Gazpacho with Basil

This simple chilled Spanish soup cropped up on so many menus in the '60s and '70s. With cartons of passata now widely available, it is easier to make than ever. We've added frozen cubes of olive oil which melt beguilingly as you sip.

PREPARATION: 15 MINUTES,
PLUS 2 HOURS' CHILLING
SERVES 6–8

about 250 ml / 9 fl oz extra-virgin olive oil

1 red onion, chopped

2 garlic cloves, finely chopped

1 red pepper, deseeded and chopped

4 tomatoes, chopped

2 slices of white bread, roughly torn

500 ml / 18 fl oz passata, or 400 g / 14 oz
    can of tomatoes liquidized with their juices

4 tbsp white wine vinegar

1 tsp Tabasco sauce

300 ml / ½ pint vegetable stock

1 tsp sugar

salt and pepper

handful of basil leaves, to garnish

1 Pour 150 ml / ¼ pint of extra-virgin olive oil into an ice cube tray and freeze.

2 Put the onion, garlic, pepper, tomatoes and bread into a food processor and blend until finely chopped but not too smooth – you need to keep some of the crunchy texture.

3 Transfer to a large bowl with the passata or canned tomatoes, 5 tablespoons of the remaining oil, the vinegar, Tabasco, stock, sugar, and salt and pepper to taste (remember that food to be served chilled needs to be more strongly seasoned). Mix thoroughly, cover the bowl with plastic film and chill for at least 2 hours or overnight. You can prepare ahead up to this point.

4 Just before serving, pour the soup into serving bowls, drop a couple of frozen olive oil cubes into each, drizzle with a little more oil and tear over some basil leaves.

Caldo Verde

This traditional Portuguese soup is great for using up any leftover vegetables.

PREPARATION: 10 MINUTES,
PLUS OVERNIGHT SOAKING
COOKING: 1¼ HOURS
SERVES 4

100 g / 3½ oz dried cannellini beans

1 tbsp olive oil

1 onion, chopped

2 garlic cloves, crushed

1 large potato, diced

2 large fresh sage leaves, shredded

about 175 g / 6 oz Savoy cabbage, shredded

425 ml / ¾ pint vegetable stock

salt and pepper

1 Soak the beans overnight in cold water.

2 Drain and put in a large pan with 1.2 litres / 2 pints of cold water. Bring to the boil and boil rapidly for 10 minutes. Remove any scum with a slotted spoon. Reduce the heat and simmer for 40 minutes until the beans are tender.

3 Meanwhile, heat the oil in a pan and fry the onion and garlic for 5 minutes until softened. Stir in the potato and sage and fry for a further 5 minutes, stirring occasionally.

4 Stir the onion mixture into the beans, together with the cabbage and stock. Bring to the boil and simmer for 15 minutes, stirring occasionally. Season to taste and serve with crusty bread.

Chinese Broth with Curly Kale 'Seaweed'

PREPARATION: 15 MINUTES

COOKING: 40 MINUTES

SERVES 4

2 garlic cloves, chopped

2 lemon grass stalks, chopped

2.5 cm / 1 inch piece of fresh ginger root, chopped

5 spring onions, sliced

1 red chilli, deseeded and chopped

1.4 litres / 2^1/$_2$ pints vegetable stock

1 tbsp chilli or olive oil

85 g / 3 oz baby sweetcorn, halved lengthwise

2 small carrots, cut into matchsticks

140 g / 5 oz curly kale, shredded

100 g / 4 oz button mushrooms, quartered

250 g / 9 oz pack of fresh Chinese noodles, or 125 g / 4^1/$_2$ oz dried

1 tbsp dry sherry

2 tbsp soy sauce

2 tbsp lime juice

vegetable oil, for frying

salt and pepper

1 Place the garlic, lemon grass, ginger, spring onions and chilli in a food processor and blend to a coarse paste. Heat the stock in a pan with the paste until boiling. Reduce the heat, cover and simmer for 30 minutes.

2 Meanwhile, heat the oil in a wok or large frying pan, add the sweetcorn, carrots and 100 g / 4 oz of the kale and cook for 5 minutes. Add the mushrooms and stock mixture and cook for a further 3 minutes. Add the noodles and cook for 2 minutes (4 if using dried). Stir in the sherry, soy sauce and lime juice and simmer for a further 1 minute. Season to taste.

3 Heat about 2 cm / ^{3}/$_4$ inch of vegetable oil in a frying pan. Add a little of the remaining kale to the pan, if it sizzles it is hot enough. Add the rest of the remaining kale and fry for a few seconds. Remove with a slotted spoon and drain on absorbent kitchen paper; it should become crisp.

4 Serve broth and noodles in bowls, topped with crispy kale.

Spiced Lentil Soup with Lemon Yoghurt

PREPARATION: 15 MINUTES

COOKING: 50 MINUTES

SERVES 4

sprig each of parsley, coriander and thyme

1 celery stalk

3 tbsp olive oil

2 medium onions, chopped

2 medium carrots, chopped

5 garlic cloves, roughly chopped

1 tbsp ground cumin

1 tbsp paprika

2 tsp ground turmeric

500 g / 1 lb 2 oz puy lentils

2.25 litres / 4 pints vegetable stock

juice of $1/2$ lemon

150 ml / $1/4$ pint double cream

25 g / 1 oz butter

salt and pepper

FOR THE LEMON YOGHURT:

100 ml / $3^1/2$ fl oz Greek-style yoghurt

2 tbsp chopped fresh coriander

grated zest of 1 lemon

1 Tuck the herbs into the hollow side of the celery stalk and bind with string to make a bouquet garni.

2 Heat the oil in a large pan and fry the onions, carrots, garlic and spices for 5 minutes, stirring to prevent burning.

3 Add the bouquet garni, lentils and stock. Bring to the boil and simmer, covered, for 40–45 minutes, stirring occasionally, until the lentils are tender. Discard the bouquet garni.

4 Process until smooth in a blender or food processor. (You may need to do this in batches.) Return to the clean pan and reheat gently. Stir in lemon juice, cream and butter. Season.

5 Make the lemon yoghurt: mix the yoghurt with half the coriander and half the lemon zest. Divide the soup between 4 bowls and add a spoonful of the lemon yoghurt to each. Scatter the remaining coriander and lemon zest over to serve.

Simple Curried Vegetable Broth

PREPARATION: 20 MINUTES

COOKING: 20–30 MINUTES

SERVES 4

1 tbsp olive oil

1 medium onion, finely chopped

2 celery stalks, chopped

1 large potato, chopped

2 carrots, chopped

1 parsnip, chopped into large chunks

2 tbsp mild curry paste or garam masala

1 tbsp plain flour

850 ml / $1^1/2$ pints vegetable stock

2 tbsp double cream

salt and pepper

FOR THE GARNISH:

knob of butter

1 large onion, thinly sliced

2 tbsp chopped fresh coriander

1 Heat the oil in a large pan and add the vegetables. Toss well and cook for 3–4 minutes until lightly browned.

2 Stir in the curry paste or garam masala and the flour and mix together well. Pour over the stock and bring to the boil. Simmer, stirring occasionally, for 20–30 minutes until the vegetables are tender.

3 Meanwhile, prepare the garnish: heat the butter in a frying pan and gently cook the onion for 7–10 minutes until browned.

4 Stir the cream into the soup, adjust the seasoning and serve immediately, sprinkled with the fried onion and chopped coriander.

Mushroom Wonton Soup

PREPARATION: 25 MINUTES, PLUS 30 MINUTES' CHILLING
COOKING: 15 MINUTES
SERVES 4

140 g / 5 oz plain flour, plus more for dusting

1 tsp caster sugar

2 tbsp sesame oil

1 tsp white wine vinegar

3 tbsp warm water

35 g / 1$\frac{1}{4}$ oz dried shiitake or other mushrooms

150 ml / $\frac{1}{4}$ pint boiling water

175 g / 6 oz fresh chestnut mushrooms

bunch of spring onions

2 tbsp soy sauce

1.2 litres / 2 pints vegetable stock

$\frac{1}{2}$ small red chilli, thinly sliced

2.5 cm / 1 inch piece of root ginger, grated

2 garlic cloves, thinly sliced

2 tbsp dry sherry

groundnut oil, for brushing

85 g / 3 oz egg thread noodles

175 g / 6 oz pak choi or spinach, shredded

1 Mix flour, sugar, sesame oil and vinegar with enough warm water to make a firm dough. Knead lightly and chill for 30 minutes.
2 Soak the dried mushrooms in the boiling water for 10 minutes. Drain, reserving the liquid. Place half the mushrooms in a food processor with two-thirds of the chestnut mushrooms, half the spring onions and 1 tablespoon of the soy sauce. Blend to a paste.
3 On a lightly floured surface, roll dough very thinly to a 30 cm / 12 inch square. Trim and cut into sixteen 7.5 cm / 3 inch squares. Spoon a little mushroom paste into the centre of each. Bring one corner diagonally over filling and seal edges to form little triangles.
4 Bring the stock and mushroom liquid to the boil in the base of a steamer, then add the remaining mushrooms and spring onions, sliced, shiitake, soy sauce, chilli, ginger, garlic and sherry.
5 Oil steaming rack and arrange wontons in a single layer. Cover and steam for 10 minutes. Add noodles and pak choi to soup. Re-position wontons and cook 3-5 minutes more until tender.
6 Serve the soup and noodles in bowls, topped with the wontons.

Jane Grigson's Spicy Parsnip Soup

PREPARATION: ABOUT 20 MINUTES

COOKING: ABOUT 30 MINUTES

SERVES 4

1 heaped tbsp coriander seeds

1 tsp each cumin seeds and turmeric

1 dried chilli, or $^{1}/_{2}$ teaspoon dried chilli flakes

$^{1}/_{4}$ teaspoon ground fenugreek

1 medium onion, chopped

1 large garlic clove, split

2-3 large parsnips, cut up

2 heaped tbsp (about 50 g / 2 oz) butter

1 tbsp plain flour

1 litre / 2 pints beef stock

150 ml / $^{1}/_{4}$ pint single cream

chopped chives or parsley, to garnish

1 Grind the coriander and cumin seeds, turmeric, chilli flakes and fenugreek in a spice grinder or electric coffee mill, or pound them in a mortar. Put the mixture into a small jar – you will not need it all for this recipe, but can use it up flavouring lentils or spinach.

2 Cook the onion, garlic and parsnip gently in the butter, in a covered pan, for 10 minutes. Stir in the flour and 1 tablespoon of the spice mixture. Cook for 2 minutes, giving the whole thing a stir from time to time. Pour in the stock gradually and leave to simmer. When the parsnip is really tender, purée in the blender, then return to the pan and dilute to taste with water.

3 Reheat, add the cream and adjust the seasoning. Serve scattered with chives or parsley. Croutons of bread fried in butter can be served as well.

Vegetable Stock

This stock makes an excellent base for any soup. It keeps, covered, in the refrigerator for up to a week or frozen for 1 month. If you reduce it down for a sauce, don't add any salt.

PREPARATION: 15 MINUTES

COOKING: ABOUT 1¼ HOURS

MAKES ABOUT 3 LITRES / 5¼ PINTS

1.8 kg / 4 lb mixed vegetables, preferably
    including carrots, onions, celery stalks and
    tomatoes, coarsely chopped

large handful of parsley, chopped

1 garlic clove, halved (optional)

1 small red chilli (optional)

1 bay leaf

1 tsp black peppercorns

salt

1 Put all the ingredients except the salt in a large pot, add 4 litres / 7 pints of cold water and bring to the boil.

2 Reduce the heat to a gentle simmer and cook gently, uncovered, for about 1 hour.

3 Strain through a fine sieve, discarding the solids, and season to taste with salt.

NOTE: The inclusion of leek and cabbage adds body to the stock, but be sure not to use too much of any one vegetable or it will overpower the others.

Velvety Cauliflower Cheese Soup

PREPARATION: 15 MINUTES

COOKING: ABOUT 40 MINUTES

SERVES 6

1 large cauliflower (750–900 g / 1 lb 10 oz–
    2 lb), broken into large florets

salt and pepper

85 g / 3 oz butter

1 medium Spanish or white mild onion,
    chopped

700 ml / 1¼ pints semi-skimmed milk

3 tbsp single cream

1 rounded tbsp plain flour

chopped fresh parsley, to garnish

FOR THE TOPPINGS:

6 sheets of rice paper (about 15 x 20 cm/
    6 x 8 inches)

150 g / 5½ oz Gruyère cheese, finely grated

1 tbsp vegetable oil

2 tsp black mustard seeds

1 Preheat the oven to 200°C / 400°F / gas 6. Reserve about 140 g / 5 oz of the cauliflower, then blanch the rest in a pan of boiling salted water for 2–3 minutes. Drain well.

2 Melt the butter in a pan, then fry the onion for 4 minutes until it is softened but not browned. Add the blanched cauliflower and cook for 2 minutes. Add the milk and 300 ml / ½ pint of water and bring to the boil. Reduce the heat and simmer for 20 minutes, until the cauliflower is tender and soft.

3 Meanwhile, make the toppings: lay 3 sheets of rice paper on each of 2 large baking sheets. Scatter over the cheese to give a fairly even coverage. Bake for about 10 minutes, until the cheese is melted and light golden. Don't allow it to turn dark brown or it will develop a bitter taste. When cooler, break into large pieces, set aside.

4 Break the reserved cauliflower into tiny florets. Heat the vegetable oil in a small non-stick pan until hot, then fry these florets until light brown. Add the mustard seeds and shake the pan until the seeds pop and release their flavour. (Take care, some of the seeds may jump out of the pan.)

5 In a small bowl, mix the cream and flour to a paste. Add a spoonful of the hot soup, stir well, then add the mixture back to the soup and cook gently, stirring, until slightly thickened. Season, then purée in a blender until smooth and creamy.

6 Spoon into warmed soup bowls, sprinkle with stir-fried cauliflower and mustard seeds and the cheesy rice cracker pieces, and garnish with parsley.

Minty Pea and Ham Soup

Mint freshens up an old favourite. This soup needs a quality stock, so a cube just won't do this time.

PREPARATION: 15 MINUTES

COOKING: ABOUT 20 MINUTES

SERVES 4

50 g / 2 oz butter

about 100 g / 4 oz leeks, very thinly sliced

500 g / 1 lb 2 oz frozen peas

250 g / 9 oz ham from the bone, cubed small

2 litres / 3½ pints good (preferably home-
    made) chicken or vegetable stock

salt and pepper

1 tbsp shredded fresh mint, plus a few sprigs
    for garnish

1 Melt the butter in a pan and gently sauté the leek for 3–4 minutes. Add the peas and ham, and toss together.

2 Add the stock, bring to the boil and simmer for 15 minutes. Season to taste.

3 Purée half the soup in a blender until very smooth; return to the pan with the remaining soup. Mix well, then add the mint and heat through.

4 Spoon some soup into each of 4 warmed bowls and garnish with mint sprigs.

With potatoes and onions, tomatoes have become the most ubiquitous vegetables – on sale all year round and relatively inexpensive. In fact, they are so much at the heart of so many cuisines, it is hard to believe that they were only brought to Europe from the Americas just a few centuries ago. Unfortunately, as with any food-stuff made so readily available, quality and flavour seem to have been sacrificed for convenience. It's therefore worth trying some of the new varieties on offer to find tasty specimens. As with most 'vegetable fruits', flavour is largely a function of ripeness, and the best indication of ripeness is a good deep (usually red) colour.

Tomatoes should be kept at room temperature – the low temperatures of the fridge masks any flavour. Perfectly ripe specimens will keep for a day or two; under-ripe ones for up to a week. If they've gone beyond perfectly ripe to become very soft and squashy, don't discard them. Although unsuitable for slicing for salads and sandwiches, etc., they will still have bags of flavour if cooked, say in a sauce.

Unless cooking tomatoes whole or halved (as in stuffing), or in a dish to be sieved or puréed, it is usually best first to remove the skins as they otherwise become stringy. Pop the tomatoes in a bowl, pour over boiling water and let stand for 20 seconds. Drain and refresh with cold water. The skins should then come away with ease.

Tomatoes

Old-fashioned Tomato Sauce

A classic tomato sauce is easy enough to buy, but a home-cooked version tastes so much better. We've kept this sauce simple, so nothing competes with the flavour of the tomatoes – but, if you want to zap it up, add your own favourite flavourings. This makes about 700 ml / 1¼ pints.

1 Skin and deseed 1.35 kg / 3 lb ripe tomatoes; roughly chop the flesh. Heat 3 tablespoons of olive oil in a heavy pan, add 1 small chopped onion and 1 finely chopped garlic clove and cook gently for 4–5 minutes until soft but not brown.
2 Add the tomatoes and cook, covered, over a medium heat for 25–30 minutes, stirring often. Towards the end of this time, add 1 tablespoon fresh or frozen oregano (or 1 teaspoon dried). When the sauce is ready, the tomatoes will have broken down to produce a thick sauce consistency. Season to taste. If the sauce needs a little more sweetness, stir in up to ½ teaspoon of sugar.
3 Pour into a lidded glass or plastic container and store in the fridge. Use within 3–4 days.
4 For a smoother consistency (to serve with spaghetti, say), sieve the finished sauce – just don't skin the tomatoes in step 1. Do deseed them, though, or the rich flavour will be diluted.

Jerusalem Artichoke Soup

Jerusalem artichokes are among the unsung heroes of the vegetable world and make this most delicious of soups. It can happily be prepared ahead, or frozen at the end of step 3.

PREPARATION: 25 MINUTES
COOKING: 50 MINUTES
SERVES 8
25 g / 1 oz butter
2 onions, sliced
800 g / 1 lb 12 oz Jerusalem artichokes
600 ml / 1 pint vegetable stock (or potato cooking water)
salt and white pepper
pinch of sugar
600 ml / 1 pint milk
2 tbsp single cream, to finish
croutons, to serve

1 Heat the butter in a large heavy-based pan. Add the onions, cover and let them sweat for 5 minutes until soft but not brown.
2 Peel and slice the Jerusalem artichokes, then add them to the softened onions for about 15 minutes, or until they are just tender.
3 Pour in the vegetable stock or potato cooking water and season with salt, white pepper and the sugar. Bring to the boil. Lower the heat and simmer for about 20 minutes until soft.
4 In a blender or food processor, liquidize the soup mixture in batches, then pour this purée back into the clean pan together with the milk.
5 Bring the soup gently back to just below the boil, then stir in the cream.
6 Serve with croutons.

Chilled Beetroot Soup with Horseradish Cream

This brilliantly coloured soup tastes just as vivid as it looks and really couldn't be easier to make. We recommend using a blender rather than a food processor, for a smoother finish.

PREPARATION: 15 MINUTES
SERVES 4
1 orange
350 g / 12 oz cooked beetroot
425 ml / $^3/_4$ pint organic vegetable juice
225 g / 8 oz Greek-style yoghurt
salt and pepper
1 tbsp horseradish sauce
fresh mint sprigs, to garnish
good crusty bread, to serve

1 Using a zester, remove the rind from half the orange (or thinly pare off the rind with a potato peeler and shred it finely). Place in a cup with just enough boiling water to cover and allow to stand for at least 10 minutes to soften. Finely grate the remaining rind and squeeze the juice from the orange.
2 Place in a blender with the beetroot and vegetable juice. Blend until smooth. Blend in half the yoghurt and season to taste. Chill until ready to serve.
3 Add the horseradish sauce to the remaining yoghurt. Pour the chilled soup into 4 individual serving bowls. Add a spoonful of the horseradish mixture to each. Drain and pat dry the softened orange rind and then scatter this over the cream. Garnish with the mint sprigs and serve with some good crusty bread.

Chickpea and Tomato Broth

Serve with a green salad as a starter or light lunch.

PREPARATION: 10 MINUTES
COOKING: 20–25 MINUTES
SERVES 4

1 tbsp sunflower oil

1 onion, chopped

500 g / 1 lb 2 oz floury potatoes, cut into 1 cm / ¹/₂ inch cubes

1¹/₂ tbsp curry paste or powder

700 ml / 1¹/₄ pints vegetable stock

400 g / 14 oz can of tomatoes

425 g / 15 oz can of chickpeas, drained

175 g / 6 oz frozen peas

squeeze of lemon juice

salt and pepper

TO SERVE:

warm naan bread

natural yoghurt

1 Heat the oil in a large heavy-based pan. Cook the onion and potatoes, stirring, for 3–4 minutes.

2 Stir in the curry paste or powder and the stock. Bring to the boil, then simmer for 10–15 minutes.

3 Add the tomatoes with their liquid, the chickpeas and peas. Simmer for 5 minutes.

4 Season with a little lemon juice, salt and pepper. Ladle into bowls and serve with naan bread and some natural yoghurt in a separate bowl.

Making Overtures

Vegetables make the best of starters and light meals, providing delicious flavours and intriguing textures to tease the palate, while staying light and healthy – packed full of nutrients. Try them in combination with tasty cheeses, in fluffy omelettes and soufflés, or crisp tartlets; alternatively you can deliver all their crunch in piquant salads.

Starters, Snacks and Light Meals

Feta and Anchovy Stuffed Peppers

Instead of red peppers you could use yellow or orange peppers. As a change from feta, you could use another crumbly cheese, such as good old British Wensleydale or a sharp goats' cheese.

You can roast the peppers up to a day ahead, cover and chill. Remove from the fridge 30 minutes before serving.

PREPARATION: 15 MINUTES
COOKING: 30 MINUTES
SERVES 6
3 red peppers
85 g / 3 oz can of anchovies, drained
1 garlic clove, finely chopped
200 g / 8 oz cherry tomatoes, quartered
2 tbsp olive oil
2 tsp balsamic vinegar
salt and pepper
140 g / 5 oz feta cheese
a few fresh basil leaves, shredded

1 Preheat the oven to 190°C / 375°F / gas 5. Quarter the peppers, deseed them and put in a single layer in a roasting tin, skin-side down. Cut the anchovies into 24 strips (you get about 10 in this size of can, so halve most of them and cut a couple of the larger ones into three).
2 Mix together the garlic, tomatoes, oil, vinegar and salt and pepper to taste, then spoon a little of this mixture into the cavity of each pepper. Arrange two anchovy strips crossed on each.
3 Bake the peppers for 25–30 minutes, until tender. Leave them to cool.

4 Slice the feta thinly, then break it into pieces. Put two pepper pieces on each plate and drizzle over the pan juices. Sprinkle with the crumbled feta and shredded basil.

New Vegetables à la Grecque

You could use crisp fresh mangetout or sugar snap peas instead of the broad beans.

PREPARATION: 15 MINUTES
COOKING: 25 MINUTES
SERVES 4
5 tbsp olive oil
1 large garlic clove, crushed
3 baby aubergines or 1 small aubergine
   (about 85 g / 3 oz), chopped into small dice
1 red (or ordinary) onion, thinly sliced
1 large tomato, skinned and chopped
3 tbsp sun-dried tomato paste
2 tbsp red wine vinegar
salt and pepper
450 g / 1 lb baby new potatoes, scrubbed
   and halved
350 g / 12 oz baby carrots, halved
450 g / 1 lb broad beans, shelled
115 g / 4 oz young asparagus spears
TO SERVE:
25 g / 1 oz black olives
1 tbsp capers
flat-leaf parsley leaves
crusty bread

1 Heat the olive oil in a frying pan, then add the garlic, aubergine and onion and cook over a moderate heat until very soft, about 10 minutes.
2 Transfer the mixture to a very large bowl and stir in the chopped tomato and sun-dried tomato paste. Add the red wine vinegar and season to taste with salt and pepper.
3 Cook the potatoes and carrots in a pan of lightly salted boiling water for about 15 minutes until tender, then drain well. Meanwhile, steam the broad beans and asparagus for about 5 minutes until just tender.
4 While they are still hot, tip the vegetables into the aubergine mixture. Stir well to coat and leave to cool for about 5 minutes before serving so they absorb the flavours of the sauce.
5 Serve sprinkled with black olives, capers and parsley leaves, and accompanied by good crusty bread.

Baked Goats' Cheese Parcels with Sweet-and-sour Leeks

This recipe from Peter Gorton looks spectacular but, surprisingly, most of the ingredients are simple store-cupboard basics. The goats' cheese parcels and the beetroot dressing can be prepared the day before and kept covered in the fridge. The tomato garnish can be made up to 2 hours in advance.

PREPARATION: 30 MINUTES

COOKING: 15 MINUTES

SERVES 4

8 sheets of filo pastry (each about
  33 × 18 cm / 13 × 7 inches)

55 g / 2¹/₂ oz butter, melted

175 g / 6 oz Valscombe soft rindless goats'
  cheese (or any, soft, rindless goats' cheese)

55 g / 2¹/₂ oz mixed shelled hazelnuts and
  pistachios, roughly chopped

salt and pepper

FOR THE BEETROOT DRESSING:

55 g / 2¹/₂ oz cooked beetroot, chopped

¹/₄ tsp Dijon mustard

1 tbsp red wine vinegar

¹/₂ tsp sugar

4 tbsp olive oil

FOR THE SWEET-AND-SOUR LEEKS:

4 tbsp olive oil

2 garlic cloves, crushed

2 tsp caster sugar

1 kg / 2¹/₄ lb leeks, trimmed and cleaned, cut
  in half lengthwise and then into chunks

juice of 1 lemon

FOR THE TOMATO GARNISH:

1 medium tomato

2 tbsp olive oil

2 tsp fresh mixed herbs (such as flat-leaf
  parsley, thyme and oregano)

1 Working quickly before the pastry dries and keeping all but the sheet you are working on under a damp tea towel, place a sheet of filo on a flat surface and brush it all over with a little of the melted butter. Place the second sheet on top and cut in half to make 2 squares. Brush one with a little more butter and place the other stack on top at an angle to create an eight-pointed star. Butter the top layer of pastry. Repeat to make 4 stacked pastry stars.

2 Cut the goats' cheese into 4 equal pieces and shape each piece into a ball. Place a cheese ball in the centre of each filo star. Sprinkle over the nuts, then season. Bring together the corners of each star and twist to make a bundle. Place on a baking sheet and brush with the remaining butter. Chill until required.

3 Preheat the oven to 200°C / 400°F / gas 6. To make the beetroot dressing: place all the ingredients in a food processor with 3 tablespoons water and blend until smooth. Set aside until required.

4 To make the Sweet-and-sour Leeks: heat the oil in a large pan. Add the garlic and sugar and stir until the sugar caramelizes. Add the leeks and sprinkle with the lemon juice. Cover and simmer for 4–5 minutes.

5 Meanwhile, bake the filo parcels for 5 minutes until golden and crispy at the edges.

6 Make the tomato garnish: cut the tomato into quarters and scoop out the seeds. Run a sharp knife underneath the flesh of the each tomato quarter to remove the skin. Cut each quarter into 4 strips and toss in the oil and herbs.

7 To assemble: place a small mound of the leeks in the middle of each plate and place a goats' cheese parcel on top. Spoon round the beetroot dressing and decorate each plate with the tomato garnish.

Feta and Herb Briouats

A brioaut *is the Moroccan name for stuffed pastries made with* warka, *the local wafer-thin pastry. However, this version from Lindsey Bareham uses filo pastry instead.*

PREPARATION: 50 MINUTES

COOKING: 30–40 MINUTES

SERVES 6

50 g / 2 oz butter or 2–3 tbsp olive oil

3 onions, halved and thinly sliced

1 tsp salt

1/2 tsp ground cinnamon

5 medium eggs, beaten

2 tbsp coarsely chopped flat-leaf parsley

1 1/2 tbsp coarsely chopped fresh
    coriander

85 g / 3 oz feta cheese, diced

salt and pepper

FOR THE PASTRY:

12 sheets (about 400 g / 14 oz) filo pastry

50 g / 2 oz melted butter or 4 tbsp olive oil

FOR THE RED PEPPER AND

TOMATO SAUCE:

400 g / 14 oz jar of sweet red peppers (pimentos)

400 g / 14 oz jar of chopped tomatoes

pinch of saffron strands, softened in a little
    boiling water

1 tbsp clear honey

2 garlic cloves, crushed

squeeze of lemon juice

1 Heat about half the butter or olive oil in frying pan over a moderate heat. Stir in the thinly sliced onions and sprinkle with the salt. Cook for a few minutes, then cover the pan and cook, stirring occasionally, until the onions are quite soft but not coloured.

2 Stir in the ground cinnamon, beaten eggs and the remaining butter or olive oil. Keep over a low heat for 2–3 minutes until the eggs are thickened but still moist (like scrambled eggs). Stir in the chopped herbs and the feta, and season. Transfer to a bowl and allow to cool.

3 Make the Red Pepper and Tomato Sauce: drain the peppers and put them in a blender or food processor with the tomatoes, saffron, honey, salt and pepper. Blend this mixture to a purée. Pour into a pan, add the garlic and simmer for 30 minutes until quite thick and reduced by about half.

4 Meanwhile, preheat the oven to 180°C / 350°F / gas 4. Working as quickly as you can, take a sheet of the filo pastry (keep the rest of them under a damp tea towel so they don't dry out) and brush half of one side down the length with the melted butter or olive oil. Fold this over to make a long strip, then paint the folded surface with some more butter or oil. Cut the sheet in half across its width.

5 Place a good teaspoon of the feta mixture on the bottom of each half of buttered pastry, fold over the edges, brush the surface of the pastry with some more melted butter or oil, then roll it up like a plump spring roll. Brush with yet more melted butter or oil and place on an oiled baking sheet, seam-side down. Repeat to make 24 pastries.

6 Bake the pastry rolls for 20–25 minutes until golden. Finish the sauce by seasoning to taste with the lemon juice and more salt and pepper if necessary. Serve it with the hot briouats.

Aubergine and Mozzarella Stacks

These Mediterranean towers will bring sunshine flavours to your table at any time of year. Serve with garlic bread. You can make this dish ahead; make the stacks up to the end of step 2, then cover and chill for up to 24 hours. Make the sauce, cover and chill for up to 2 days.

PREPARATION: 20 MINUTES
COOKING: 20–25 MINUTES
SERVES 6

1 medium aubergine
2 tbsp olive oil, plus more for the dish
150 g / 5½ oz pack of mozzarella cheese
6 slices of prosciutto
handful of basil leaves, torn, to serve
FOR THE SAUCE:
350 g / 12 oz jar of crushed tomatoes, or 400 g / 14 oz can
   of chopped tomatoes and 2 tsp tomato purée
2 tbsp extra-virgin olive oil
1 garlic clove, chopped

1 Preheat the oven to 200°C / 400°F / gas 6 and the grill to high. Cut 12 slices of aubergine about 1 cm / ½ inch thick. Arrange these over the grill pan in one layer and brush with half the olive oil. Grill for 3–4 minutes until well browned; turn, brush and grill again. Allow to cool.
2 Cut the mozzarella into 6 slices. Sandwich each between two aubergine slices. Put the 'sandwiches' in a greased shallow ovenproof dish, crumple the prosciutto on top and bake for 12–15 minutes until the cheese melts.
3 While they are cooking, make the sauce: put all the ingredients in a pan and simmer briefly (or until slightly thickened, if using canned tomatoes). Spoon a little sauce on each plate, put the stacks on top and scatter with basil.

Robert Carrier's Tomato Stacks

PREPARATION: ABOUT 25 MINUTES

SERVES 4 (EASILY HALVED)

70 g / 2¾ oz packet of mixed salad leaves

1 large red onion, finely chopped

6 tbsp finely chopped flat-leaf parsley

6 tbsp finely chopped coriander leaves

4 large ripe tomatoes

FOR THE VINAIGRETTE:

150 ml / ¼ pint extra-virgin olive oil

juice of 1 large juicy lime, or 2 tbsp fresh lemon juice

2 garlic cloves, finely chopped

1 tsp Dijon mustard

salt and pepper

pinch of crushed dried chillies

FOR THE GARNISH:

sprigs of basil, coriander and flat-leaf parsley

black olives

1 First make the vinaigrette: in a small bowl, whisk together the oil, citrus juice, chopped garlic and mustard. Season with plenty of salt, pepper and a pinch of dried chillies. Set aside.
2 Tear half the salad leaves into small pieces and put in a bowl, then mix in the onion, parsley and coriander. Spoon over the vinaigrette, toss, cover with film and chill until ready.
3 Cut a thin slice off the bottom of each tomato so it will stand up when stacked. Cut each tomato widthwise into 5 even slices – reassemble each tomato as you do, so you know which slices belong to which tomato.
4 Stir the red onion salsa so it is well mixed. Put the bottom slice of one tomato on a chilled salad plate. Spoon over a little salsa, season with salt and pepper, then place the second slice on top. Repeat the layers to complete the stack, then repeat with the other three tomatoes.
5 Arrange a few olives, the rest of the salad leaves and fresh herb sprigs around each plate. Drizzle any remaining salsa over the salad. Garnish each tomato with one or two parsley leaves and an olive. Serve immediately.

Vegetable Patties with Spicy Tomato Chutney

These vegetarian patties from Clare Gordon-Smith are made from a base of sweet potato, with the addition of grated courgettes and grated carrots.

PREPARATION: 15 MINUTES, PLUS 30 MINUTES' STANDING

COOKING: ABOUT 30 MINUTES

SERVES 4

350 g / 12 oz courgettes

salt and pepper

550 g / 1¼ lb sweet potatoes

200 g / 7 oz carrots

1 green Thai chilli

1 spring onion

2 tbsp natural yoghurt

flour, for dusting

vegetable oil, for frying

FOR THE SPICY TOMATO CHUTNEY:

4 tomatoes

1–2 red chillies

2 tbsp chopped fresh mint

1 tbsp cider vinegar

pinch of sea salt

1 First make the chutney: roughly chop the tomatoes, finely chop the chillies, then mix both with the mint, vinegar and salt. Set aside until ready to serve.
2 To make the patties: first grate the courgettes, sprinkle them with salt and set aside for 30 minutes to draw out some of the watery juices. Meanwhile, boil the sweet potatoes until tender, drain and mash them. Grate the carrots, deseed and chop the chilli and slice the spring onion. Rinse the courgettes, drain well and pat dry.
3 Mix the vegetables, yoghurt, salt and pepper in a bowl. With floured hands, shape the mixture into 8 patties.
4 Heat a shallow layer of oil in a heavy-based pan and fry the patties for 4 minutes on each side.
5 Serve the patties with the spicy chutney.

Honeyed Carrot and Fig Couscous

This Persian-style dish can be made using bulgar wheat instead of couscous, if you prefer. For an extra tangy flavour, cook the carrots in fresh fruit or vegetable juice.

PREPARATION: 10 MINUTES, PLUS STANDING
COOKING: 20 MINUTES
SERVES 4

4 tbsp clear honey
finely grated zest and juice of 1 lemon
850 ml / 1¹/₂ pints vegetable stock
450 g / 1 lb baby carrots, trimmed
350 g / 12 oz couscous
1 tsp garlic purée
1 pomegranate
3 ripe figs, quartered
2 tbsp chopped fresh flat-leaf parsley
1 tbsp chopped fresh mint
salt and pepper

1 Place the honey, lemon zest and juice in a large shallow pan with 300 ml / ¹/₂ pint of the stock. Stir and bring to the boil. Add the carrots and simmer over a very low heat for 10 minutes. Bring back to the boil and boil for 8 minutes, until the liquid is thick and caramelized.

2 Meanwhile, place the couscous in a shallow dish. Mix the remaining vegetable stock and garlic purée together and pour over the couscous to cover. Leave to stand for 10 minutes until all the liquid has been absorbed.

3 Scoop the seeds and pulp from the pomegranate. Fluff up the couscous and toss with the pomegranate, figs and herbs. Season and serve with the carrots and remaining syrup.

Goats' Cheese Polenta with Mushrooms

This deliciously glamorous starter also makes a good quick supper dish. Use instant polenta because it cooks so quickly and a firm goats' cheese – look out for chèvre logs. Both are now available from most large supermarkets.

PREPARATION: 5 MINUTES
COOKING: 10 MINUTES
SERVES 4

450 ml / 16 fl oz dry white wine
1 tsp salt
85 g / 3 oz butter, cut into pieces
175 g / 6 oz instant polenta
175 g / 6 oz firm goats' cheese, rind removed, cubed
3 tbsp olive oil
225 g / 8 oz mixture of wild and chestnut mushrooms, trimmed and cut into pieces
300 g / 10 oz packet of young leaf spinach
50 g / 2 oz Cheddar cheese, grated
4 spring onions, finely shredded, to garnish

1 Put the wine in a large pan with an equal quantity of water and bring to the boil. Stir in the salt and butter, stirring until the butter melts. Add the polenta in a steady stream, whisking constantly until cooked (usually about 2 minutes, but check the instructions on the packet). Remove from the heat and stir in the goats' cheese. The polenta should be soft in consistency and spoonable.

2 In a pan, heat 1 tablespoon of the oil, then fry the mushrooms for 2 minutes; remove and set aside. Fry the spinach in two batches, each in a tablespoon of olive oil, until just wilted – but no longer than 1 minute.

3 Spoon the goats' cheese polenta into wide serving bowls and pile up the spinach and mushrooms in the centre. Scatter with grated Cheddar and shredded spring onions and serve immediately.

Warm Salad of Roasted Aubergine, Tomatoes and Cannellini Beans

PREPARATION: 30 MINUTES

COOKING: ABOUT $1^1/_2$ HOURS

SERVES 6 AS A STARTER OR 4 AS A SNACK

1 large, or 2 small, aubergine, about 350 g / 12 oz in weight

900 g / 2 lb tomatoes

$^1/_2$ garlic bulb, halved vertically, top trimmed but cloves left unseparated

2 red chillies

2 tsp clear honey

6 tbsp olive oil

salt and pepper

175 g / 6 oz dried cannellini beans, cooked, or a 400 g / 14 oz can

boiling water

generous pinch of saffron threads

2 tsp red wine vinegar

1 heaped tbsp finely chopped fresh parsley

1 Preheat the oven to 160°C / 325°F / gas 3. Cut the aubergine into 5 cm / 2 inch thick rounds and quarter them. Cut a cone from the top of each tomato to remove the core, then cut the tomatoes in half, or quarter them if large.

2 Arrange the aubergine pieces, tomatoes, garlic and chillies in a roasting tin. Drizzle over the honey and olive oil, and season. Roast for $1^1/_2$ hours, basting occasionally.

3 Remove and discard the chillies. Squeeze the garlic from its skin back into the vegetables. Spoon the vegetables into a serving dish, leaving the juices in the tin. Plunge the cannellini beans into boiling water until hot, then drain and pat dry on kitchen paper. Add the beans to the vegetables and stir well.

4 Grind the saffron in a mortar, then blend with 2 teaspoons of boiling water. Add to the roasting tin with the vinegar and stir until blended. Season to taste, then pour over the vegetables and beans. Scatter over the parsley and serve warm.

Vegetable Omelette

PREPARATION: 15 MINUTES
COOKING: 15–20 MINUTES
SERVES 4

4 tbsp olive oil

1 onion, sliced

1 garlic clove, finely chopped

1 aubergine, cut into chunks

2 courgettes, cut into chunks

2 tomatoes, cut into wedges

salt and pepper

6 eggs

$^{1}/_{4}$ tsp dried oregano

handful of fresh basil leaves (optional)

green salad, to serve

1 Heat the oil in a frying pan with a heatproof handle. Add the onion and cook until softened. Add the garlic, aubergine and courgette chunks, and cook for 5–8 minutes until softened and slightly brown. Add the tomato wedges and season with salt and pepper.

2 Meanwhile, beat the eggs in a bowl, stir in the dried oregano and season. Preheat the grill.

3 Pour the beaten eggs over the vegetables and cook for 5–8 minutes, until the bottom is starting to brown and the eggs look softly set.

4 Slide the omelette under the grill and cook until the top looks puffed and golden.

5 Tear over the basil leaves, if using, then cut the omelette into wedges and serve with a green salad.

Asparagus is now available all year round, but it is at its best during the few weeks in May and June when our own British asparagus is in season.

When buying, look for firm unwrinkled stalks, and beware of any with wet cut ends as that probably means that they have been standing in water to try to refresh them. Also check that ready-packed bunches don't hide inferior, or much smaller or misshapen, stalks in their centres. If buying loose stalks, try to choose ones of roughly the same thickness so that they will all cook at the same rate.

If you want to, you can keep your asparagus stalks fresh at home by standing them in water, but it is much better to use them fairly swiftly.

To prepare asparagus, first remove the woody stems from a point just above where it starts to feel softer to the touch. All but the youngest and most tender of stems are also much improved by light peeling of the stringy outer skins.

Asparagus is most usually steamed or boiled; traditional asparagus kettles allow the stalks to be boiled while the tips steam more gently at the top. Recently it has become fashionable to roast or griddle asparagus stalks briefly after painting the stalks very lightly with olive oil or melted butter.

Asparagus

Asparagus with Lime and Coriander Butter

This citrus butter gives a super zesty kick to any simple steamed vegetable, noodles or even jacket potatoes. It will keep in the fridge for 2 weeks and in the freezer for 1 month.

1 First make the Lime and Coriander Butter: place 50 g / 2 oz softened butter in a bowl with the zest and juice of 1 lime and 2 tablespoons of chopped fresh coriander. Beat together until smooth. Spoon on greaseproof paper and roll up to form a log shape. Twist the ends of the paper to seal and place in the fridge until firm.

2 Trim 900 g / 2 lb fresh young asparagus spears and peel as appropriate (see introduction). Steam for 10–15 minutes until just tender. Drain well and pat dry.

3 Cut the chilled log of flavoured butter into slices and serve with the warm asparagus.

Asparagus and Soft Egg Tartlets

Served with a green salad this makes a great starter or light lunch.

PREPARATION: 15 MINUTES
PLUS 30 MINUTES' CHILLING
COOKING: 35 MINUTES
MAKES 4

FOR THE PASTRY:

100 g / 4 oz plain flour

50 g / 2 oz butter, cut into small pieces

1 small egg

FOR THE FILLING:

100 g / 4 oz thin asparagus

salt and pepper

4 eggs

2 tbsp single cream

1 tbsp finely grated Parmesan or mature
  Cheddar cheese

a little freshly grated nutmeg

1 Make the pastry: tip the flour into the food processor, add the butter, then process until it resembles fine crumbs. Throw in the egg and work briefly to form a dough. Tip the dough on to a lightly floured surface and knead briefly. Wrap in plastic film and chill for half an hour.

2 Preheat the oven to 200°C / 400°F / gas 6. Cut the asparagus into 5 cm / 2 inch lengths. Bring a large pan of salted water to the boil, throw in the asparagus and cook for 5 minutes. Drain and cool quickly in cold water.

3 Divide the dough into 4 equal pieces. Roll out each piece and use to line four 10 cm / 4 inch tartlet tins or a 4-hole Yorkshire pudding tin. Trim off the excess pastry with a sharp knife. If using tins, set them on a baking sheet. Line each pastry case with a round of greaseproof paper and half fill with baking beans or uncooked rice. Bake for 12–15 minutes, then remove the paper and beans and bake for 3–4 minutes more, until the pastry is crisp and light golden.

4 Divide the asparagus between the tartlets, then break an egg into each. Drizzle over the cream and sprinkle with the grated cheese, nutmeg, salt and pepper. Return to the oven for 5–8 minutes until the egg is just set and the top lightly browned.

5 Serve warm or cold.

Roasted Asparagus with Poached Eggs

PREPARATION: 10 MINUTES
COOKING: 20–25 MINUTES
SERVES 6

450 g / 1 lb thin asparagus spears

25 g / 1 oz butter

50 g / 2 oz fresh white breadcrumbs

salt and pepper

grated zest of 1 lemon

3 tbsp freshly chopped parsley

olive oil, for brushing and drizzling

150 ml / 1/4 pint white wine vinegar

6 very fresh eggs

Parmesan shavings, to serve

1 Preheat the oven to 200°C / 400°F / gas 6. There is no need to peel the asparagus, but if it is thick, snap off any woody stems at the point where they break easily.

2 Melt the butter in a pan and fry the breadcrumbs, stirring often, until crisp. Remove from the heat. Season, then stir in lemon zest and parsley.

3 Lay the asparagus on an oiled baking sheet and brush them with oil. Roast for 12–15 minutes.

4 Meanwhile, half-fill a medium pan with water, add the vinegar and bring to the boil. Crack in the eggs from a height of about 10 cm / 4 inches (this gives them a good round shape). Simmer until the white is firm (3–4 minutes). Using a slotted spoon, transfer to a bowl of warm water (they will keep warm this way for up to 30 minutes).

5 Arrange the asparagus on plates. Drizzle with more oil and scatter over the Parmesan shavings. Spoon the eggs on top and sprinkle with the crumbs. Season with coarse sea salt and black pepper.

Things on Toast

SPICY AVOCADO ON CORIANDER CORNBREAD TOAST

SERVES 4

Toast 4 thick slices of cornmeal (or white) bread on both sides, splash over some extra-virgin olive oil and sprinkle with some sea salt. Scoop teaspoons of flesh from 2 avocados and arrange these on the toast. Squeeze over some fresh lemon or lime juice. Add a splash of Tabasco sauce, more salt and olive oil, pepper, and a handful of coarsely torn coriander leaves.

ROAST HAM AND MUSHROOM TOAST

SERVES 4

Preheat the oven to 220°C / 425°F / gas 7. Mix 4 tablespoons olive oil with 1 finely chopped garlic clove. Arrange 4 large flat mushrooms, stalks removed, in a roasting tin and brush with a little of this garlic oil. Top each mushroom with a slice of ham and a quarter of a deseeded red pepper, and brush all over with a little more garlic oil. Sprinkle with salt and pepper and roast for about 15 minutes until the mushrooms are just starting to soften.

Meanwhile, brush 4 large thick slices of white bread on both sides with the remaining garlic oil. Put these on a baking sheet and bake for about 15 minutes. Remove the mushrooms from the oven and top each with a thin slice of Stilton. Return to the oven for about 5 minutes more.

To serve, put a stuffed mushroom on each piece of toast and drizzle with the juices from the roasting tin.

FIELD MUSHROOMS WITH TRUFFLE OIL ON ITALIAN COUNTRY TOAST

SERVES 4

Thickly slice 6 large field mushrooms and toss with about 10 wild mushrooms or pre-soaked dried porcini slices. In a frying pan, heat a little olive oil and fry a chopped garlic clove and the mushrooms for 5–6 minutes. Stir in 4 tablespoons of crème fraîche and a pinch of cayenne. Under a moderate grill, toast 4 slices of Italian country bread on both sides. Pile the mushroom mixture on top and drizzle over a little truffle oil.

ROAST VINE TOMATOES AND ONIONS WITH CHEDDAR

SERVES 4

Preheat the oven to 220°C / 425°F / gas 7. In an ovenproof frying pan, heat 2 tablespoons of olive oil, then fry 8–12 peeled baby pickling onions sprinkled with 2 teaspoons of sugar for about 5 minutes, until tinged golden brown. Add $1^{1}/_{2}$ tablespoons of white wine vinegar and cook for 4–5 minutes until reduced. Preheat a hot grill.

Add 225 g / 8 oz baby vine tomatoes on their stems to the pan, then transfer the pan to the oven and roast for 8 minutes.

Toast 4 thick slices of farmhouse white bread on both sides, then place on a baking sheet. Sprinkle with olive oil, salt and pepper. Top with the onion and tomato mixture and drizzle over any juices left in the pan. Sprinkle with basil leaves and Cheddar shavings, season again, and place under the hot grill until the cheese has melted.

Garlicky Mushroom Toasts

In autumn, you may find wild mushrooms, such as girolles, chanterelles and ceps, in the shops. Add just a few and the chestnut mushrooms will take on that lovely wild flavour.

PREPARATION: 10 MINUTES
COOKING: 15 MINUTES
SERVES 6

1 tbsp olive oil

2 garlic cloves, crushed

450 g / 1 lb mixed mushrooms, such as
    chestnut and oyster, sliced

3 tbsp Marsala, Madeira or sweet sherry

284 ml / 10 fl oz carton of double cream

salt and pepper

FOR THE TOASTS:

1 ciabatta loaf, cut into three chunks

50 g / 2 oz butter, softened

4 tbsp chopped fresh parsley, plus more
    for garnish

1 Make the toasts: preheat the grill and split each ciabatta chunk in half. Grill on the crust sides. Mix the butter and parsley; spread this over the cut sides of the ciabatta.

2 Cook the mushrooms: heat the oil in a large frying pan. Add the garlic and mushrooms and fry over a fairly high heat for 6–7 minutes, turning occasionally. Cook until the liquid evaporates.

3 Pour the liquor into the pan and bubble for a few minutes. Stir in the cream and season with salt and pepper.

4 Toast the cut side of the ciabatta until the butter is melted and golden. Put on plates, spoon over the mushrooms, season with black pepper and garnish with more chopped parsley.

Goats' Cheese and Olive Toasts

PREPARATION: 10 MINUTES
COOKING: 8 MINUTES
MAKES 20

10 thin slices of white bread, crusts removed

1 tbsp green olive pâté

1 tbsp black olive pâté

1 tbsp sun-dried tomato paste

225 g / 8 oz soft rindless goats' cheese,
    such as Capricorn

2 tbsp chopped fresh parsley

FOR THE BASIL DRESSING:

3 tbsp olive oil

1 tbsp balsamic vinegar

1 tbsp finely chopped fresh basil

salt and pepper

1 Preheat the oven to 200°C / 400°F / gas 6. Spread each slice of bread with one of the olive pâtés or the sun-dried tomato paste. Spread each of them now with a little of the cheese (warming the cheese for a few seconds in the microwave makes it much easier to spread). Roll each slice up tightly, secure with 2 cocktail sticks and arrange, spaced well apart, on a baking tray.

2 Make the Basil Dressing: whisk the ingredients together well until emulsified. Season to taste.

3 Brush the toasts with the dressing and sprinkle over the parsley. Cook in the oven for 8 minutes, until crisp and golden.

4 Remove the cocktail sticks and cut each toast into 2 equal pieces. Arrange on a serving plate and serve warm or cold.

Potato Cakes with Swiss Chard and Hollandaise

The potato cakes and hollandaise sauce can be made a day in advance, and the dish assembled in minutes.

PREPARATION: 30 MINUTES
COOKING: 15 MINUTES
SERVES 4
175 g / 6 oz floury potatoes, cut into large chunks
3 tbsp crème fraîche
3 medium eggs, separated
25 g / 1 oz Parmesan cheese, grated
1 tbsp olive oil
FOR THE HOLLANDAISE:
2 large egg yolks
1 tbsp white wine vinegar
2 tbsp lemon juice
175 g / 6 oz butter, melted
1 tsp wholegrain mustard
FOR THE TOPPING:
50 g / 2 oz butter
140 g / 5 oz Swiss chard, shredded
140 g / 5 oz wild mushrooms (e.g., shiitake, chanterelles), sliced
8 spring onions, shredded
1/4 tsp freshly grated nutmeg
salt and pepper

1 Cook the potatoes in boiling water for 6–8 minutes until just tender. Drain and leave to cool.
2 To make the hollandaise, place the egg yolks and a pinch of salt in a food processor and process. In a pan, bring the vinegar and lemon juice just to the boil. With the motor still running, gradually add the lemon juice and vinegar to the egg yolks. Slowly pour in the melted butter and process until thickened. Transfer to a bowl and stir in the mustard. Place the bowl in a pan of hot water to keep warm.
3 Coarsely grate the potatoes. Stir in the crème fraîche, egg yolks and Parmesan. Season.

4 In a large bowl, whisk the egg whites until they form soft peaks. Using a metal spoon, beat a little egg white into the potato mixture to loosen it, then fold in the rest.
5 Preheat the grill to moderate. Heat the oil in a large non-stick frying pan. Lightly oil four 3 cm / 1 1/4 inch deep, 9 cm / 3 1/2 inch plain round pastry cutters. Place the cutters in the pan and fill three-quarters full with the potato mixture. Fry for 1 minute until the base is cooked. Place the pan under the grill and cook for a further minute until the tops are golden and set. Keep warm.
6 For the topping: melt the butter in a large frying pan, add the chard, mushrooms, spring onions and nutmeg and cook for 1–2 minutes. Season to taste.
7 Remove the cutters from the potato cakes and transfer to plates. Spoon the veg on top and drizzle the sauce over.

Tricolor Muffins

This snack is great served warm.

PREPARATION: 10 MINUTES
COOKING: ABOUT 15 MINUTES
SERVES 4
4 muffins
1 aubergine, thickly sliced
2 tbsp garlic-flavoured oil
1 large beef tomato, thickly sliced
4 tbsp crème fraîche
4 tsp ready-made pesto sauce
handful of rocket or watercress

1 Split the muffins in half and lightly toast them, if you like.
2 Fry the aubergine slices in the garlic-flavoured oil until crisp and blackened.
3 Place a slice of aubergine on each muffin base, followed by a thick slice of beef tomato and a spoonful of crème fraîche. Spoon over some of the pesto sauce and finish with some fresh rocket or watercress.
4 Top carefully with the muffin lids to serve.

Cherry Tomato and Basil Clafoutis

Traditional clafoutis *is a lightly cooked batter dessert studded with cherries – rather like a soft, slightly custardy Yorkshire pudding. This savoury version, using ripe cherry tomatoes, Parmesan and basil, works beautifully. Serve it as a starter, or as a light lunch with a crisp salad.*

PREPARATION: 10 MINUTES
COOKING: 20 MINUTES
SERVES 6

butter, for greasing
650 g / 1 lb 7 oz cherry tomatoes
4 eggs
25 g / 1 oz plain flour
200 ml / 7 fl oz carton of crème fraîche
4 tbsp milk
good handful of fresh basil, roughly torn
50 g / 2 oz Parmesan cheese, grated
salt and pepper

1 Preheat the oven to 190°C / 375°F / gas 5. Lightly grease six 2.5 cm / 1 inch deep, 13 cm / 5 inch gratin dishes with butter and spread the tomatoes over the bases. Beat the eggs in a large bowl, then beat in the flour using a wire whisk. Beat in the crème fraîche and the milk until the batter is smooth. Stir in the basil and all but one tablespoon of the Parmesan. Season.
2 Pour the batter over the tomatoes and sprinkle with the remaining cheese and an extra grinding of pepper. Bake for 20 minutes until puffed up and golden on top.
3 Serve warm with a green salad.

VARIATION: To make one large clafoutis for a lunch dish to serve 3–4 people, put 450 g / 1 lb small tomatoes in a 4 cm / 1½ inch deep, 23 cm / 9 inch ceramic dish, then follow the recipe above but bake for 30–35 minutes.

Tarragon Mushrooms with Bean Mash

PREPARATION: 15 MINUTES
COOKING: 20 MINUTES
SERVES 4

1 tbsp olive oil
1 large Spanish onion, sliced
2 tbsp cornflour
600 ml / 1 pint vegetable stock
6 tbsp dry sherry
8 medium field mushrooms
sprig of fresh tarragon, stalks removed
3 large potatoes, diced
1 garlic clove, thinly sliced
400 g / 14 oz can of flageolet beans, drained
    and rinsed
3 spring onions, finely chopped
3 tbsp milk
salt and pepper

1 Heat the olive oil in a large frying pan and fry the onion for 2–3 minutes until softened slightly.
2 Mix the cornflour with a little of the vegetable stock to make a thin smooth paste. Stir into the remaining stock, with the sherry, and pour over the onions. Bring to the boil and simmer, stirring constantly, for 2–3 minutes, until thickened.
3 Push the mushrooms under the surface of the gravy. Sprinkle over the tarragon and simmer for 10 minutes.
4 Meanwhile, cook the diced potatoes and garlic in lightly salted boiling water for 8 minutes. Add the flageolet beans and cook for a further 2 minutes. Drain and mash. Stir in the spring onions and milk. Beat until smooth and season to taste.
5 Serve immediately, with the tarragon mushrooms and sauce spooned over them.

Gary Rhodes' Warm Poached Eggs on Potato Salad

PREPARATION: 25 MINUTES
COOKING: ABOUT 20 MINUTES
SERVES 4

150 ml / ¼ pint white wine vinegar or malt vinegar

4 eggs

handful each of rocket and baby spinach leaves

1 tbsp olive oil

FOR THE POTATO SALAD:

450 g / 1 lb new potatoes

1 tbsp olive oil

juice of 1 lime

1 tbsp finely chopped shallot

2–3 tbsp crème fraîche

FOR THE GREEN BUTTER:

25 g / 1 oz sorrel leaves, finely shredded or 1 tbsp chopped tarragon

50 g / 2 oz butter, softened

squeeze of fresh lemon juice (a little more if you're using tarragon)

coarse sea salt and pepper

1 Bring a large pan of water to a simmer and add the vinegar. One at a time, break the eggs into a cup and gently slip them into the pan. Cook for 3 minutes, then, using a slotted spoon, transfer immediately to a bowl of iced water.
2 Make the potato salad: cook the potatoes for about 15 minutes until tender. Drain, peel and mash roughly with a fork. Stir in the remaining ingredients and season. Mix well.
3 Make the green butter: mash the herbs with the butter, lemon juice, and season, then set aside (do not chill).
4 Sit a 7.5 cm / 3 inch ring mould on each plate and spoon in the potato, pressing down well (or spoon a neat mound on the plate). Toss the rocket and spinach in the olive oil and season. Lay across the potato or scatter around the edge.
5 Bring a pan of water to a simmer. Remove the eggs from the iced water and carefully neaten with scissors. Plunge into the simmering water for 1 minute to reheat. Sit them on the potato bases, spoon over the butter and serve sprinkled with salt.

Grilled Sweet Potato and Beetroot Salad

You can also cook the sweet potato on the barbecue until deliciously charred and tender – perfect for warm days when you want to dine alfresco.

PREPARATION: 20 MINUTES
COOKING: 20 MINUTES
SERVES 4

900 g / 2 lb sweet potatoes, unpeeled

salt and pepper

2 tbsp olive oil

700 g / 1 lb 9 oz fresh cooked baby beetroot, halved

50 g / 2 oz rocket leaves

1 tbsp pine nuts, toasted

FOR THE DRESSING:

2 tsp horseradish cream

4 tbsp soured cream

2 tbsp chopped fresh dill

1 Preheat the grill. Slice the sweet potatoes into rounds about 1 cm / ½ inch thick, then cut each round in half again. Lightly sprinkle each slice with salt and pepper. Brush with the oil and place under the grill. Grill the potatoes for 10 minutes on each side until tender. For the final 5 minutes of cooking, add the beetroot to the grill pan and toss in the oil. (To avoid the colour from the beetroot bleeding into the potato, move the potato slices to one end of the grill.)
2 Arrange the rocket leaves either in a large serving dish or on individual plates. Mix the dressing ingredients together until thoroughly combined, then season to taste. Top the rocket leaves with the potato slices and beetroot halves, then drizzle the dressing over the top. Scatter over the pine nuts and serve immediately.

Piedmontese Peppers

For this recipe a hot oven is absolutely essential to cook the peppers and tomatoes to a tender texture and sweet flavour. Serve the peppers hot or cold, scattered with the fresh herbs, or add a few teaspoons of capers and chopped stoned black olives.

PREPARATION: 10 MINUTES
COOKING: 15–20 MINUTES
SERVES 2

2 red peppers
2 garlic cloves, sliced
2 plum tomatoes, halved
2 tbsp extra-virgin olive oil
salt and pepper
handful of fresh basil leaves, roughly chopped
1 tbsp roughly chopped fresh oregano

1 Preheat the oven to 220°C / 425°F / gas 7. Halve the peppers and remove the seeds but not the stalks. Place the peppers skin-side down on a lightly oiled baking sheet. Place slices of garlic inside each pepper half and top each with a plum tomato half, cut-side down. Drizzle with the oil, season and bake for 10 minutes.
2 Reduce the oven setting to 200°C / 400°F / gas 6 and continue baking for a further 15–20 minutes, until the peppers and tomatoes are tender.
3 Serve hot or cold, scattered with the fresh herbs.

Warm Maple-glazed Vegetable Salad with Feta and Walnuts

This simple hot salad makes an interesting light supper, served with warm walnut bread. You can assemble the parcels in advance, ready for last-minute steaming.

PREPARATION: 15 MINUTES
COOKING: 30 MINUTES
SERVES 4

350 g / 12 oz small new potatoes
115 g / 4 oz baby onions or shallots
140 g / 5 oz feta cheese, cubed
100 g / 4 oz frozen broad beans
115 g / 4^1/$_2$ oz baby corn, halved lengthwise
100 g / 4 oz sugar snap peas
50 g / 2 oz walnut pieces, lightly toasted
grated zest of 1 orange
3 tbsp roughly chopped fresh parsley
2.5 cm / 1 inch piece of root ginger, grated
salt and pepper
5 tbsp maple syrup
2 tsp olive oil

1 Steam the potatoes and onions or shallots in a steamer rack set over boiling water in the base of a steamer for about 20 minutes until just tender. Reserve the water for later use.
2 Cut four 33-cm / 13-inch circles from greaseproof paper. In a bowl, toss the potatoes and onions with the feta, broad beans, corn, sugar snap peas, walnuts, orange zest, parsley, ginger and seasoning. Divide between the circles of paper.
3 Mix together the syrup and oil and spoon over the veg. Bring the paper up over the filling and twist together to seal.
4 Place the parcels in the steamer rack, cover and steam for 10 minutes. To test that the vegetables are just tender, unwrap one parcel and pierce the vegetables. If necessary, re-wrap and steam for a little longer.
5 Serve in the parcels.

Freshness is paramount when buying beans; any showing signs of limpness or wrinkling are definite rejects. Look for smooth, firm specimens that snap cleanly when bent. Runner beans should not be discoloured or coarse. Yard-long beans should be a bright grassy green. Don't worry about brown flecks on yard-longs – these are part of the pigmentation and will disappear during cooking. Beans in prime condition will keep for 3–4 days in a plastic bag in the fridge.

If your beans need stringing, snap off both ends, pulling them back along the length of the bean to remove the strings; or in the case of runner beans, use a swivel peeler. If the beans are stringless, line them up a handful at a time and chop off the stem ends. You can remove the slender growing tips of French beans if you wish. Leave beans whole if they seem tender enough; otherwise cut them into short lengths.

For maximum flavour, steam your beans. Otherwise, drop them into a large pan of boiling salted water and cook for 3–10 minutes, depending on variety and preferred degree of doneness. Drain thoroughly and sizzle in melted butter just before serving.

Beans

Salted Runner Beans

Salting runner beans works brilliantly as a preservative and an alternative to freezing – the result is crisp, fresh beans throughout the autumn and winter.

1 Wash, top and tail 1.3 kg / 3 lb beans and cut into 2.5 cm / 1 inch diagonal slices.
2 Sprinkle a 1 cm / $^1/_2$ inch layer of coarse sea salt into a wide-necked 1 litre / 1$^3/_4$ pint glass jar. Cover with a 2.5 cm / 1 inch layer of beans and repeat until the jar is full.
3 Push the beans down to pack tightly and cover the jar with waxed paper. Loosely secure with string and leave for 2 days.
4 After 2 days, the beans will have settled. Add more layers, cover with waxed paper, seal with a non-metallic lid; keep in a cool dark place for up to 6 months.
5 To use, remove the amount of beans you need and rinse in a colander under cold running water. Soak in plenty of fresh water for 2 hours. Drain, rinse and cook by boiling for 4 – 5 minutes until tender.

Vegetable Salad with Curry-soy Vinaigrette

This delightful warm vegetable salad has a bold dressing. The idea is French, but the enticing flavours are exotically Asian.

PREPARATION: 10 MINUTES
COOKING: 10 MINUTES
SERVES 4

225 g / 8 oz ripe tomatoes
100 g / 4 oz broccoli, cut into small florets
100 g / 4 oz French beans, trimmed
100 g / 4 oz cauliflower, cut into small florets
100 g / 4 oz podded fresh or frozen peas
50 g / 2 oz fresh water chestnuts, peeled and sliced
3 tbsp finely chopped shallots, squeezed dry
3 tbsp finely snipped chives
FOR THE CURRY-SOY VINAIGRETTE:
2 tsp Dijon mustard
2 tsp Madras curry powder
2 tbsp light soy sauce
2 tsp salt, or to taste
1 tsp freshly ground five-pepper mixture or black pepper
4 tbsp extra-virgin olive oil

1 First make the vinaigrette: combine the ingredients well in a bowl. Set aside.
2 Drop the tomatoes into a pan of boiling salted water for 5 seconds, then remove them with a slotted spoon. Skin them and remove the seeds. Cut the flesh into 4 cm / 1½ inch pieces and set aside.
3 Add the broccoli, beans and cauliflower to the pan and cook for 3 minutes. Add the peas and cook for 1 minute more. Drain the vegetables, tip into a warm bowl and add the tomatoes and water chestnuts.
4 Drizzle in the vinaigrette, add the shallots and chives. Mix well to serve.

Three-bean Salad with Citrus Dressing

This colourful starter or side dish is easily turned into a main course by adding a 400 g / 14 oz can of tuna chunks, well drained, or 225 g / 8 oz feta cheese cubes. Its fabulous flavour is enhanced by using toasted sesame oil – or you could try hazelnut or walnut oil instead.

PREPARATION: 20 MINUTES
COOKING 8 MINUTES
SERVES 4

225 g / 8 oz runner beans
225 g / 8 oz French beans, halved
450 g / 1 lb broad beans or fresh peas, shelled
bunch of spring onions, sliced
8 radishes, halved
1 tbsp chopped fresh chives
juice and finely grated zest of 1 small orange
3 tbsp olive oil
salt and pepper
1 tbsp toasted sesame oil
150 ml / ¼ pint Greek-style yoghurt
2 tbsp chopped fresh mint

1 Top and tail the runner beans and remove the strings; cut into 2.5 cm / 1 inch slices and cook in boiling salted water for 4 minutes. Add the French beans and broad beans or peas and cook for 4 minutes until just tender. Drain and refresh in cold water.
2 Tip the beans into a large bowl and add the spring onion, radishes and chives. Mix together the orange juice, oils and salt and pepper, then tip this over the vegetables and toss.
3 Mix together the orange zest, yoghurt and mint. Divide the bean salad between plates and spoon some of this citrus dressing on top.

Salad Dressings

What do you put on a salad before tossing it? A dressing vinaigrette, French dressing, French vinaigrette, or a vinaigrette dressing? Just a few terms for what is basically the same thing. And once you've conquered a basic dressing, you can head off in all sorts of flavour directions.

Just scan any aisle of ready-made dressings and you'll see the potential – from sun-dried tomato, Caesar-style, and Italian, to zesty garlic, lime and dill, honey and mustard, Parmesan, sesame and ginger, and toasted onion.

You can easily make all these and more, for a fraction of the price and with a better flavour.

MIXING THE DRESSING

The neatest and easiest way is to measure your ingredients into a jar, seal with a lid and shake vigorously like a cocktail; this makes the oil and vinegar emulsify into a glossy thickish liquid. The jar should have a wide neck or you'll have to use a funnel, and it should be roomy so the contents get thoroughly mixed.

It also needs to fit comfortably in your hand (so you can shake it easily) and should have a secure lid, preferably with a screw-top. After shaking, the dressing gradually separates out but will emulsify again in a couple of shakes.

Dressings are best made fresh, but you can chill any left over for up to 3 days – bring the dressing to room temperature before using as the oil thickens, even solidifies, in the fridge.

Not all dressings have to be mixed before use. If you sprinkle the oil and vinegar separately over the plate, you can create a pretty pattern. Use different flavoured and coloured oils and vinegars, such as raspberry vinegar with walnut oil. A few drops of balsamic vinegar contrasts well with a flavoured olive oil.

For mixed leaves, dressings must be tossed in just before serving so the leaves retain their crispness. Italian cooks don't always bother to mix the dressing at all – they just squeeze some lemon juice over the leaves, drizzle over the oil, then toss together. Another idea is to pour the dressing into the salad bowl – or even mix it in the bowl – drop the leaves on top and toss.

TRANSFORMING DRESSINGS

Before taking your basic dressing a step further, consider what it is going to be poured over or tossed with. The flavours should blend harmoniously, and not clash or overpower each other.

Green leaves benefit from a sprinkling of chopped herbs, such as chives, parsley or tarragon. Be braver with stronger-flavoured vegetables, meat or fish – add creamed horseradish, crushed garlic, finely chopped capers or anchovies, or a robust mustard.

Change the flavour and texture of a dressing completely with piquant blue cheeses such as Stilton, Roquefort or Danish blue and serve with a mixture of salad leaves and toasted nuts, such as hazelnuts or walnuts, and chicken. (Use a lighter oil than olive with cheese.)

Then there are creamy dressings made with half dressing and half mayonnaise, soured cream or yoghurt. Their smoothness makes them ideal for spooning over warm new potatoes and beans, cold poached chicken or salmon. Vary creamy dressings and add colour and texture by whizzing them in a food processor with fresh herbs, watercress, roasted red peppers or skinned and seeded tomatoes.

Dressings can be served warm. Either add warm cooking juices to the vinaigrette, as in a chicken liver salad or seafood salad, or heat the dressing in the pan you used for cooking (for instance if you've been frying prawns, chicken or bacon). A particularly delicious classic warm dressing is Sauce Vierge (right).

MAKING A PERFECT DRESSING

There are no set rules about which oils and vinegars to use. A basic dressing is three parts oil to one part vinegar or lemon juice (this is just a guide – some people tone down the vinegar by adding more oil), and salt and pepper to taste.

WHICH OIL?

Olive oil is the traditional choice, but you can lighten its taste by mixing it with a milder-flavoured one, such as sunflower. If you decide to use a stronger-flavoured oil, such as walnut or hazelnut, you may want to tone it down by mixing with a blander oil like groundnut.

WHICH VINEGAR?

Red or white wine and the sweet balsamic are the most popular, but try other flavoured varieties if the dish warrants it. Tarragon vinegar, for example, goes well with a chicken salad, while fruit vinegars, such as raspberry and blackcurrant, are beautiful in a warm dressing for roast meats, particularly game.

ANYTHING ELSE?

You can add a teaspoon of mustard or cream to help the oil and vinegar combine, but it's not essential. Some chefs add a few drops of water to delay the vinegar hitting the palate before the softer oil; it certainly makes a sharp dressing taste milder.

SAUCE VIERGE

Heat 4 tablespoons olive oil, 1 tablespoon wine vinegar and 8 lightly crushed coriander seeds to infuse. Toss in 4 finely chopped tomatoes (skinned and seeded) and 1 tablespoon each chopped chervil, parsley and tarragon. Cook very briefly and spoon over grilled prawns or scallops, or lightly steamed vegetables.

Dandelion Leaves with Pear, Roquefort and Hazelnuts

The creaminess of the blue cheese contrasts well with the bitterness of the leaves, and the crunch of the hazelnuts.

PREPARATION: 15 MINUTES
SERVES 4

1 ripe conference pear

1 tsp fresh lemon juice

1 head of radicchio, coarsely chopped

1 head of chicory, leaves separated and ripped

handful (about 40 g / 1 1/2 oz) of dandelion
 leaves or watercress

100 g / 4 oz Roquefort or other blue cheese

2 tbsp hazelnut oil

2 tbsp extra-virgin olive oil

4 tsp balsamic vinegar

salt and pepper

50 g / 2 oz toasted hazelnuts, roughly chopped

1 Peel the pear, halve and core it, then cut the flesh into 5-mm / 1/4-inch dice. Toss with the lemon juice to stop the pear discolouring and set aside.

2 Put the radicchio, chicory and dandelion leaves or watercress in a large serving bowl. Add the pear dice, then crumble over the cheese.

3 Whisk the two oils with the balsamic vinegar. Season with salt and pepper, then pour over the salad.

4 Sprinkle with the nuts and toss everything together to serve.

Puy Lentil Salad

The lentils will absorb the wonderful flavours from the dressing. You can use larger green lentils instead of Puy, but be careful not to overcook them.

PREPARATION: 15 MINUTES
COOKING: 30 MINUTES
SERVES 8

250 g / 9 oz Puy lentils, rinsed
1 red onion, cut into thin wedges
1 red pepper, deseeded and diced
bunch of flat-leaf parsley, chopped
FOR THE DRESSING:
100 ml / 3¹/₂ fl oz virgin olive oil
3 tbsp cider vinegar
2 tsp tamari soy sauce
2 tsp Dijon mustard
2 small garlic cloves, crushed
salt and pepper

1 First make the dressing: mix together all the ingredients and set aside.
2 Place the lentils in a pan, cover with water, bring to the boil and boil rapidly for 5 minutes. Reduce the heat and simmer for 20 minutes until just tender.
3 Drain the lentils thoroughly and return to the pan. Stir in the dressing ingredients. Leave to cool, stirring occasionally, so they absorb the dressing evenly.
4 When cold, stir in the red onion, pepper and parsley. Season to taste and serve.

Tamari Toasted Seed Coleslaw

Japanese tamari soy sauce is wheat-free and very dark in colour. It has a stronger flavour than the other type of Japanese soy sauce familiar here, shoyu. Both are readily available from better supermarkets and good health-food shops.

PREPARATION: 15 MINUTES
COOKING: 3 MINUTES
SERVES 4

100 g / 4 oz mixed seeds (e.g., sunflower, sesame)
2 tbsp tamari soy sauce
1 small white cabbage (about 500 g / 1 lb 2 oz), shredded
3 medium carrots, grated
3 spring onions, finely chopped
150 ml / ¹/₄ pint mayonnaise
1 tsp whole-grain mustard
3 tbsp sunflower oil
1 tbsp white wine vinegar
salt and pepper

1 In a dry frying pan, toast the mixed seeds for 2–3 minutes, turning frequently, until lightly browned. Sprinkle over the tamari and toss together quickly. The seeds will stick together initially, but as the mixture dries the seeds will separate.
2 Combine all the vegetables in a large bowl. Mix together the mayonnaise, mustard, oil, vinegar and freshly ground black pepper. Stir into the vegetables with the cooled seed mixture and toss well. Season to taste, carefully as the tamari soy sauce is salty.

Gary Rhodes' Asparagus, Sea Kale and Red Onion Salad with Spicy Potato Croutons and Soured Cream and Chive Dressing

PREPARATION: ABOUT 30 MINUTES

COOKING: ABOUT 20 MINUTES

SERVES 4

12–16 medium asparagus spears

salt and pepper

bunch of sea kale or 4 celery stalks

4 tbsp olive or groundnut oil

$^1/_4$ tsp Madras curry powder

1 cooked jacket potato, peeled and cut into
    5 mm / $^1/_4$ inch cubes

juice of 1 lime

4–5 tbsp soured cream

1 heaped tsp very finely snipped fresh chives

2 small red onions, thinly sliced and
    separated into rings

handful of green salad leaves, such as rocket,
    spinach and watercress

12 small sorrel leaves

16–20 coriander leaves

1 Lightly peel the asparagus and trim off the woody ends, then plunge them into a deep pan of boiling salted water for 2–3 minutes, until tender. (Lift one from the water with a spoon and pinch lightly – if it is cooked, the asparagus will just start to give.) It's best to leave them with a slight bite for a better texture and flavour. Once cooked, refresh in iced water, then cut each spear diagonally into two. Remove the base of the sea kale's stalk, then leave whole or cut diagonally in half. If using celery, cut the stalks into sticks.

2 Heat 2 tablespoons of the oil in a frying pan. Sprinkle the curry powder over the potato cubes, making sure they are all evenly seasoned, then fry gently until golden and crispy. Once cooked, drain, season with a pinch of salt (reserve the oil for the dressing).

3 In a bowl, mix the remaining oil with the curried oil and a little lime juice. Place the soured cream in a separate bowl, season with salt and pepper and loosen the consistency with a little lime juice. Stir in the snipped chives.

4 Put the asparagus, sea kale, onion rings and salad leaves in a bowl, trickle over a few drops of the curried oil dressing and toss. Divide the dressed salad between serving plates and spoon some soured cream and chive dressing around the edge. Scatter the sorrel and coriander leaves and hot, crisp, spicy potato croutons over the salad. Serve immediately.

Butter Bean, Olive and Feta Salad

PREPARATION: ABOUT 15 MINUTES

SERVES 4

4 tomatoes

4 tbsp olive oil

juice of 1 lemon

two 400 g / 14 oz cans of butter beans, drained

50 g / 2 oz stoned black olives

1 small red onion, thinly sliced

200 g / 8 oz feta cheese, crumbled

handful of chopped fresh parsley

salt and pepper

1 Chop one of the tomatoes and put it in a food processor or blender with the olive oil and lemon juice; whizz until fairly smooth.

2 Cut the remaining tomatoes into wedges and mix with the beans, olives, onion, feta and parsley, then season with salt and pepper.

3 Toss in the tomato dressing and serve with pitta bread.

Mediterranean Salad

PREPARATION: 30 MINUTES

COOKING: 30–40 MINUTES

SERVES 4

2 yellow peppers, halved and deseeded

1 red pepper, halved and deseeded

3 garlic cloves, unpeeled

1 red onion, thinly sliced

$^1/_2$ cucumber, peeled and diced

6 plum tomatoes, cut into wedges

12 stoned black olives

handful of fresh basil, roughly torn

2 tbsp chopped fresh dill or parsley

1 tbsp chopped fresh oregano

salt and pepper

FOR THE ROASTED BREAD:

225 g / 8 oz firm country bread, thickly sliced and crusts removed

25 g / 1 oz butter, melted

FOR THE DRESSING:

5 tbsp extra-virgin olive oil

1–2 tbsp balsamic vinegar

1 tsp Dijon mustard

1 Preheat the oven to 200°C / 400°F /gas 6 and the grill to high. Place the peppers, skin side up, on the grill rack with the garlic cloves and cook for 10–15 minutes, turning the garlic occasionally, until the peppers are blistered and blackened all over. Push the garlic to the sides of the pan if it starts burning. When cool, peel the peppers and cut the flesh into thin strips. Place in a salad bowl.

2 Add the onion, cucumber, tomatoes, olives and herbs to the salad bowl. Season and toss lightly to mix.

3 Make the roasted bread: brush the bread on both sides with butter and cut into cubes. Arrange in a single layer on a baking sheet and bake for 10–12 minutes until golden – check frequently after 8 minutes as they colour quickly.

4 Make the dressing: peel the garlic and mash in a small bowl. Gradually whisk in the oil, vinegar, mustard and seasoning.

5 Drizzle the dressing over the salad, toss well and sprinkle over the bread cubes.

Caesar Salad with Parmesan Crisps

Many people aren't keen on the egginess of the original Caesar salad. This version removes that element from the dressing – and it still tastes great. As well as using Parmesan for the crisps, they may be made with Cheddar.

PREPARATION: 15 MINUTES

COOKING: 15–20 MINUTES

SERVES 4

5 anchovy fillets, finely chopped

1 garlic clove, finely chopped

3 tbsp olive oil

8 slices of French bread

2 sheets of rice paper

50 g / 2 oz freshly grated Parmesan cheese

1 Cos lettuce, torn into bite-sized pieces and chilled

FOR THE DRESSING:

2 tsp Dijon mustard

1 tsp sugar

1 tbsp white wine vinegar

5 tbsp olive oil

2 tbsp crème fraîche

salt and pepper

dash of Worcestershire sauce

1 Preheat the oven to 180°C / 350°F /gas 4.

2 In a bowl, mix the anchovies, garlic and oil to a paste. Spread this over each slice of bread and bake for 15–20 minutes until crisp. Cut the toasts into large bite-sized pieces.

3 Line a small baking sheet with the rice paper sheets and sprinkle them with Parmesan. Bake above the toasts for 15–20 minutes until the cheese is melted, crisp and pale golden. Allow to cool, then break into pieces.

4 Make the dressing: whisk together the mustard, sugar and vinegar, then gradually whisk in the oil. Whisk in the crème fraîche, season and add a dash of Worcestershire sauce.

5 Mix together the lettuce, toasts and Parmesan crisps, and drizzle the dressing over them. Toss well and pile on 4 plates.

The oven can help bring out the best in vegetables – and not simply as plain roasts: you can bake them slowly in rich sauces to bring out their full flavour; encase them in crisp pastry shells for a delicious texture contrast; or stuff them with a range of fillings to produce hearty warming family fare.

Putting on the Heat

Bakes, Gratins, Pies and Tarts

Macaroni Cheese Pie with Artichokes and Mushroom

Here Gary Rhodes has devised the most luscious version of macaroni cheese ever. All the elements can be prepared ahead and assembled just before serving. What makes this dish so special is the inclusion of three sauces – mornay (a cheesy white sauce), a Parmesan sauce made with cream and a Hollandaise sauce. Here you can make a shortcut by replacing the Hollandaise with two egg yolks. The recipe uses canned artichokes, but you can always use cooked fresh globe artichokes if you prefer.

PREPARATION: 20 MINUTES

COOKING: 55 MINUTES

SERVES 4

25 g / 1 oz butter, plus more for greasing

450 g / 1 lb puff or shortcrust pastry, defrosted if frozen

85 g / 3 oz macaroni, cooked, drained and cooled

200 g / 8 oz canned artichokes, drained, or 2 cooked globe artichokes

100 g / 4 oz chestnut or button mushrooms, quartered

150 ml / $^1/_4$ pint Hollandaise Sauce (page 44) or 2 egg yolks

2 heaped tbsp softly whipped cream

FOR THE MORNAY SAUCE:

15 g / $^1/_2$ oz butter

15 g / $^1/_2$ oz plain flour

200 ml / 7 fl oz milk

salt and pepper

$^1/_2$ tsp prepared English mustard

85 g / 3 oz Cheddar cheese, grated

FOR THE PARMESAN SAUCE:

285 ml / $^1/_2$ pint carton of double cream

85 g / 3 oz freshly grated Parmesan cheese

2 tbsp crème fraîche

lemon juice to taste

TO SERVE:

tossed green salad, flavoured with balsamic vinaigrette, sliced red onions, watercress and walnuts

1 Preheat the oven to 200°C / 400°F / gas 6. Lightly butter four 10 cm / 4 inch round pastry rings (6 cm / 2$^1/_2$ inches deep) and sit them on a baking sheet lined with greaseproof paper. Roll out the pastry to a thickness of about 2 mm / $^1/_{16}$ inch and cut out four 10 cm / 4 inch circles. Sit one in each ring. Roll out the remaining pastry and cut into strips wide enough to line the sides of the rings. Once in place, press the pastry along the bottom edge to seal with the base, then all the way around the sides so it comes a little above the ring.

2 Line each mould with greaseproof paper or foil and fill with baking beans or rice. Leave to rest in the fridge for 20 minutes, then bake blind for 15–20 minutes, until a light golden colour – this will guarantee a crisp finish. Remove from the oven, take out the foil and beans and set aside until ready to use.

3 To make the Mornay Sauce: melt the butter in a small pan, add the flour and cook over a low heat for a few minutes without letting it colour. Meanwhile, warm the milk in a separate pan, then gradually ladle it into the flour pan, stirring constantly to make a smooth sauce. Simmer for 20–25 minutes until thickened and smooth. Season with salt and pepper to taste. Stir in the mustard and grated cheese and heat gently, stirring, until the cheese has melted. Pass the sauce through a sieve into a bowl and cover until needed. Reheat very gently, without boiling.

4 Make the Parmesan Sauce: pour the cream into a large pan and bring to the boil. Lower the heat, then whisk in the Parmesan and crème fraîche. Add the lemon juice, salt and pepper to taste. Stir in the cooled cooked macaroni and gently warm through.

5 To assemble the pies: warm the cases in the oven and preheat a hot grill. Melt the 25 g / 1 oz butter in a frying pan. Cut the artichokes into 8–12 wedges and cook in the butter with the mushrooms for 5 minutes, until golden brown. Stir into the macaroni mixture and adjust the seasoning. Divide between the pastry cases.

6 Stir the Hollandaise sauce or egg yolks and cream into the Mornay sauce and spoon into the pies. Cook under the preheated hot grill for 3–4 minutes until dark golden. Serve immediately with a tossed salad.

Leek and Potato Hereford Pie

Little Hereford cheese tastes somewhere between Cheddar and Caerphilly; Cheddar is a good substitute in this recipe from Bill Sewell.

PREPARATION: 20 MINUTES

COOKING: 55 MINUTES

SERVES 8

85 g / 3 oz butter

675 g / 1½ lb leeks, trimmed and sliced

450 ml / 16 fl oz dry cider

450 ml / 16 fl oz double cream

2 tsp wholegrain mustard

2 medium eggs, beaten

140 g / 5 oz Little Hereford or Cheddar
   cheese, grated

450 g / 1 lb potatoes, cut into 5 mm / ¼ inch
   thick slices (no need to peel)

salt and pepper

12 sheets of filo pastry, each about
   35 × 25 cm / 14 × 10 inches

1 Preheat the oven to 180°C / 350°F / gas 4. Melt one-third of the butter in a large frying pan and cook the leeks for 6–8 minutes until softened, stirring occasionally. Add the cider, bring to the boil and boil fiercely, uncovered, until reduced by about two-thirds. Add the cream, bring back to the boil and boil fiercely for 3–5 minutes, until the sauce has reached the consistency of thick cream. Remove from the heat and stir in the mustard, eggs and cheese.

2 Meanwhile, cook the potatoes in boiling water for 3–4 minutes until tender (be sure that they are cooked, as the acidity from the cider will prevent them cooking further when added to the sauce). Drain and mix gently with the leek mixture. Season.

3 Melt the remaining butter. Use a little to brush the base of a 30 × 22 cm / 12 × 8½ inch baking dish. Place a sheet of filo pastry on top and brush with a little more butter. Repeat with 4 more sheets of pastry to cover the base and sides of the dish, overlapping the edges. Spread the filling inside, then layer another 5 sheets of pastry, in the same way as before, over the top. Fold over any overlapping pastry. Brush 2 more sheets with the remaining butter, gently scrunch, and place on top of the pie.

4 Bake for 30–40 minutes until golden.

Summer Vegetable Lattice Pie

PREPARATION: 35 MINUTES,
PLUS PROVING

COOKING: 40 MINUTES

SERVES 6

oil, for greasing

225 g / 8 oz strong plain flour

7 g sachet of easy-blend dried yeast

1 tsp light muscovado sugar

salt and pepper

150 ml / ¼ pint hand-hot water

1 medium egg, beaten, for glazing

rock salt, for sprinkling

15 g / ½ oz fresh basil, stalks removed, to serve

FOR THE FILLING:

450 g / 1 lb onions, sliced

3 garlic cloves, crushed

300 ml / ½ pint vegetable stock

15 g pack of rosemary, stalks removed

1 orange, 1 red and 1 yellow pepper,
    deseeded and cut into chunks

6 plum tomatoes, quartered and deseeded

100 g / 4 oz asparagus tips

1 Lightly oil a 30×20×2 cm / 12×8×¾ inch Swiss roll tin. Sift the flour into a large bowl and stir in the yeast, sugar and seasoning. Gradually stir in the water to form a soft dough. Turn out on to a lightly floured surface and knead for 10 minutes until smooth and elastic. Return to the bowl, cover with plastic film and leave to rise in a warm place for about 1 hour until doubled in size.

2 Meanwhile, make the filling: place the onions, garlic, stock and half the rosemary in a large pan. Bring to the boil and simmer for 15–20 minutes, stirring occasionally, until all the stock has been absorbed. Set aside.

3 Preheat the oven to 220°C / 425°F / gas 7. Turn the dough out on a lightly floured surface. Cut off one-third and reserve. Roll out the remaining dough to a 32×22 cm / 12¾×8½ inch rectangle and use to line the tin.

4 Spoon the onion mixture over the base of the dough. Scatter over the peppers, tomatoes, asparagus and black pepper. Cut the reserved dough into 8 pieces and roll each to make a long 'sausage'. Arrange in a lattice pattern over the filling and pinch the ends into the pie to seal. Brush with the egg and sprinkle over the rock salt.

5 Bake for 20–25 minutes until golden. Scatter over the basil and serve hot or cold.

Roasted Vegetable Quiche

PREPARATION: 20 MINUTES

COOKING: 1 HOUR

SERVES 6

2 medium courgettes, sliced

1 yellow pepper, deseeded and thickly sliced

1 red pepper, deseeded and thickly sliced

1 tbsp olive oil

flour, for dusting

350 g / 12 oz shortcrust pastry, defrosted if frozen

1 large egg

200 ml / 7 fl oz crème fraîche

12 fresh basil leaves

salt and pepper

1 Preheat the oven to 200°C / 400°F / gas 6. Toss the courgettes and peppers in the oil in a roasting tin, then roast for 20 minutes, stirring halfway through. Remove from the oven and set aside to cool slightly.

2 Put a 23 cm / 9 inch flan ring on a baking sheet. On a lightly floured surface, roll out the pastry to a 30 cm / 12 inch circle and place in the flan ring so the sides of the ring support the pastry. Tip the vegetables into the centre of the pastry circle, then spread out to within 5 cm / 2 inches of the edge.

3 Beat together the egg and crème fraîche, then tear in the basil and season. Pour over the roast vegetables, fold over the pastry edges and pinch the tucks in the pastry together. Bake for 40–45 minutes until the filling is set.

4 Serve warm or cold.

Provençale Tarts with Pesto Sauce

If you want to make your own puff pastry, go ahead; otherwise use a good-quality frozen pastry. This recipe of Gary Rhodes' is for 4 individual tarts, but you could make one 20-cm / 8-inch tart – in which case it will take about 45 minutes to cook. The vegetables and pastry cases can be cooked up to 2 days in advance and kept in the fridge. If you do this, warm the vegetables through before you add the egg and cream mixture. The sauce is an optional extra; if you prefer, you can serve the tart with a crisp salad.

PREPARATION: 40 MINUTES

COOKING: 1–1 1/4 HOURS

SERVES 4

225 g / 8 oz puff pastry, defrosted if frozen

15 g / 1/2 oz unsalted butter

3 tbsp olive oil, plus more for drizzling

2 large onions, sliced

2 red peppers and 2 green peppers,
  deseeded and sliced

1 garlic clove, crushed

1 egg

150 ml / 1/4 pint double cream

1 tbsp freshly grated Parmesan cheese

salt and pepper

2 courgettes, sliced diagonally

4 ripe plum tomatoes, sliced

FOR THE SAUCE:

1 tbsp ready-made pesto sauce

150 ml / 1/4 pint mayonnaise

1 Preheat the oven to 200°C / 400°F / gas 6. Roll out the puff pastry on a lightly floured surface and use to line four 10 cm / 4 inch individual flan rings or tins. Line the pastry with greaseproof paper, fill with baking beans and bake the pastry cases blind for about 15 minutes. Remove from the oven and remove and discard the paper and beans.

2 Meanwhile, heat the butter with 2 tablespoons of the oil, add the sliced onions, peppers and crushed garlic and cook for 6–8 minutes until softened. Allow to cool for a few minutes.

3 Whisk the egg with the cream, Parmesan and seasoning, then stir into the onion mixture. Cook over a gentle heat, stirring until thickened, for about 10–15 minutes. Allow to cool.

4 Heat 1 tablespoon of oil in a pan and cook the courgette slices until they are lightly browned, about 3–4 minutes. Divide the onion, pepper and garlic mixture among the tart cases. Arrange alternating rows of tomato and courgette slices on top of that.

5 Reduce the oven temperature to 180°C / 350°F / gas 4 and bake the tarts for about 20 minutes.

6 Make the sauce: mix the ready-made pesto sauce into the mayonnaise, then spoon the mixture on 4 serving plates. Remove the rings from the tarts and drizzle a little olive oil over the top of each one. Set the tarts on top of the pools of pesto sauce and serve.

VARIATIONS: You can ring the changes to obtain some striking colour combinations with these tarts: try using yellow courgettes or 1 each yellow and green, either alternating slices of different colour or making 2 differently coloured types of tart. You can use sun-dried tomato paste or black olive paste if you are not a pesto fan.

Goats' Cheese and Onion Tarts

These make a lovely starter, whether the party is for six or 26. The tarts can be assembled ahead of time and frozen, and baked when needed. To prepare ahead, make up to the end of step 3, cover and chill up to 3–4 hours ahead; or prepare up to the end of step 3, open-freeze on baking sheets, then wrap in foil and freeze for up to 3 months. To cook, first defrost on baking sheets for 2 hours.

You need a firm goats' cheese that slices easily. Try Capricorn from Somerset, which is widely available in supermarkets and has a gorgeous milky flavour.

PREPARATION: 20 MINUTES

COOKING: 35 MINUTES

SERVES 6

2 red onions, thinly sliced

2 tbsp olive oil

1 tbsp balsamic vinegar

salt and pepper

250 g / 9 oz packet of puff pastry, defrosted if frozen

2 firm goats' cheeses, each 100 g / 4 oz in weight,
    at room temperature

125 g / 4 oz bag of curly endive

2 tsp fresh lemon juice

3 tbsp olive oil

50 g / 2 oz chopped walnuts

1 Preheat the oven to 220°C / 425°F / gas 7. Fry the onions gently in the oil for 10 minutes. Add the vinegar, salt and pepper, and cook for 5 minutes until just caramelized.
2 Roll out the pastry and trim to 20 × 30 cm / 8 × 12 inches. Cut six 10 cm / 4 inch squares. Put on a damp baking sheet; score lightly 1 cm / ½ inch inside each square. Don't cut through.
3 Spread the onions within this area. Use a serrated knife to cut off the ends of the cheeses; slice each into three. Put a slice on each tart.
4 Bake for 20 minutes until the pastry puffs up. Serve with the endive tossed in the lemon juice and olive oil with some salt and pepper. Sprinkle over the walnuts to serve.

French Onion Tart

No fussing about with baking tins here – this tart is cooked on a baking sheet with the filling piled on top.

PREPARATION: 30 MINUTES
COOKING: 40–45 MINUTES
SERVES 4

2 tbsp olive oil

4 large onions, thinly sliced

2 tbsp white wine vinegar

2 tbsp light muscovado sugar

salt and pepper

flour, for sprinkling

500 g packet of frozen puff pastry, defrosted

140 g / 5 oz Cheddar cheese, grated

beaten egg or milk, to glaze

green salad, to serve

1 Preheat the oven to 200°C / 400°F / gas 6. Heat the olive oil in a large frying pan, then fry the sliced onions for about 10 minutes, stirring occasionally, until they are softened. Stir in the white wine vinegar and the muscovado sugar, then increase the heat and cook, stirring frequently, for a further 4–5 minutes until the onions turn a deep caramel colour. Season with salt and pepper and set aside to allow to cool slightly.

2 On a lightly floured surface, roll out the pastry to a 35 cm / 14 inch circle, then transfer it to a baking sheet – it may flop over the edges slightly. Sprinkle half the grated Cheddar over the pastry, leaving a 6 cm / 2½ inch border around the edge, then spoon the caramelized onions over the cheese.

3 Fold the uncovered pastry edges over the filling – aim for a home-made rustic look – and brush the rim with beaten egg or milk. Sprinkle the remaining cheese over the pastry and a little over the onions.

4 Bake for about 20–25 minutes until the pastry is puffy and golden.

5 Serve cut into wedges with a green salad.

Spinach and Gruyère Tart

This is a quick and easy way of making a tart if you don't have a suitable tart tin.

If you don't have any pesto sauce, try spreading the pastry base with black olive paste or sun-dried tomato paste instead. If you want to use frozen spinach for the tart, use half the quantity and make sure it is leaf spinach, rather than chopped. It should also be thoroughly defrosted. Squeeze out the excess moisture before using, or your pastry will become soggy.

PREPARATION: 10 MINUTES
COOKING: 15–20 MINUTES
SERVES 4

1 tbsp sunflower oil

1 red onion, finely chopped

450 g / 1 lb fresh spinach

300 g / 10 oz shortcrust pastry, defrosted if frozen

2 tbsp ready-made pesto sauce

100 g / 4 oz Gruyère cheese, grated

1 medium egg, beaten

salt and pepper

1 Preheat the oven to 200°C / 400°F / gas 6. Heat the oil in a small pan and cook the chopped onion for 4 minutes until softened. Remove from the heat. Place the spinach in a large pan with only the water from washing it that remains clinging to its leaves. Heat gently until just wilted, allow to cool, then squeeze out excess moisture.

2 Roll the pastry out to a circle about 25 cm / 10 inches in diameter and place on a greased baking sheet. Spread the pastry with the pesto sauce. Stir the cheese (reserving 1 tablespoon), red onions, egg and plenty of seasoning into the spinach. Place in the centre of the pastry, leaving a 3 cm / 1¼ inch border.

3 Fold the pastry up around the spinach mixture and pinch the edges together to hold it in place. Sprinkle over the reserved grated cheese and bake for 15–20 minutes until golden.

Tomato Tarte Tatin

Though it looks distinctly impressive, this tart is surprisingly easy to make.

PREPARATION: 15 MINUTES
COOKING: 25 MINUTES PLUS 5 MINUTES' COOLING
SERVES 4

1 tsp olive oil

large knob of butter

1 tsp caster sugar

9–10 tomatoes, halved widthwise

salt and pepper

green salad, to serve

FOR THE PASTRY:

100 g / 4 oz plain flour

50 g / 2 oz butter, chopped

50 g / 2 oz mature Cheddar cheese, grated

4 spring onions, chopped

pinch of salt

1 First make the pastry: whizz the flour, butter and cheese in a food processor to make crumbs. Add the onions and salt, and mix briefly. With the machine still running, add 2–3 tablespoons of water and process until the mixture forms a ball. Wrap in cling-film.

2 In a 22–23 cm / 8½–9 inch ovenproof pan or heavy tin, heat the oil and butter. Add the sugar and heat until caramelized, stirring it into the butter and oil. Pack the tomatoes into the pan, some cut-side up, some cut-side down, and season well. Cook over a high heat for a few minutes until the tomatoes start to colour on the underside. Remove from the heat and allow to cool.

3 Preheat the oven to 200°C / 400°F / gas 6. Roll out the pastry on a lightly floured surface until it is slightly bigger than the pan. Put the pastry over the tomatoes and tuck the edges down the sides. Bake for 15–20 minutes until the pastry is golden. Remove and allow to cool for about 5 minutes so the juices can settle, then invert on a plate so the pastry is on the bottom.

4 Serve with a green salad.

Shallot Tatin

Baby onions would work just as well as the shallots.

PREPARATION: 45 MINUTES
COOKING: 40 MINUTES
SERVES 4

1 kg / 2¼ lb shallots, peeled

25 g / 1 oz butter

1 tbsp olive oil

1 tsp cumin seeds

3 tbsp dark muscovado sugar

grated zest of ½ lemon

salt and pepper

FOR THE PASTRY:

200 g / 7 oz plain flour

pinch of salt

100 g / 4 oz butter, cubed

1 egg yolk

50 g / 2 oz walnut pieces, finely chopped

1 Preheat oven to 200°C / 400°F / gas 6. Make pastry: place flour, salt, butter and egg yolk in a bowl and, using fingertips, mix fat and egg into flour until mixture has texture of coarse breadcrumbs. Stir in nuts and 2–3 tablespoons of water – enough to form a smooth, firm dough. Knead briefly, shape into a ball, wrap in plastic film and chill while preparing filling.

2 Bring a pan of water to the boil and cook the shallots for 5 minutes. Drain and pat dry. Heat the butter and oil in an ovenproof frying pan measuring about 23–25 cm / 9–10 inches. Add the shallots and cook gently, stirring, for about 10 minutes until they start to turn golden. Sprinkle on the cumin seeds, sugar, lemon zest, about 4 tablespoons of water and seasoning. Cook for 5 more minutes, until the shallots are soft and golden, with a syrupy sauce. Remove from the heat.

3 Roll out the pastry on a floured surface to a round about 5 cm / 2 inches larger than the pan. Place it over the shallots, tucking the edges down the side of the pan. Bake for 20–25 minutes, until crisp and golden.

4 Allow the tart to cool in the pan for 5 minutes, then place a large serving plate over it and invert the tart on to it.

5 Serve warm, cut into wedges.

The Jerusalem artichoke — actually a relative of the sunflower — is generally a very underrated vegetable. Raw, the knobbly tuber has a sweet nutty flavour and can be shredded into salads, but it is more usually boiled, steamed, braised with butter, deep-fried in batter or roasted. The tubers are notoriously difficult to peel so they are often simply scrubbed or peeled after preliminary parboiling. If you do peel them raw, add some lemon juice to the soaking water as they will otherwise discolour rapidly.

They are among the most nourishing of winter root vegetables, being very rich in vitamin C and minerals like potassium and phosphorus. The flavour is considered akin to that of the globe artichoke, so they make the most magnificent soups and purées. Look for unbruised specimens with as regular a shape as possible for ease of preparation.

Jerusalem artichokes

Jerusalem Artichoke and Mushroom Dauphinoise

1 Preheat the oven to 180°C / 350°F / gas 4. Cook 675 g / 1 1/2 lb Jerusalem artichokes in lightly salted boiling water for 7–10 minutes until just tender.
2 Meanwhile, heat 2 tablespoons olive oil in a large pan and fry 1 sliced onion and 2 crushed garlic cloves for 3 minutes until softened. Increase the heat, add 350 g / 12 oz sliced chestnut mushrooms and cook for a further 5–6 minutes, tossing occasionally, until golden.
3 Drain the artichokes and refresh under cold running water, drain again and then peel. Cut any large artichokes in half and arrange in a shallow 1.2 litre / 2 pint ovenproof dish with the mushroom mixture.
4 In a bowl, mix together 200 ml / 7 fl oz crème fraîche, 150ml / 1/4 pint single cream, 1 tablespoon wholegrain mustard, a pinch of grated nutmeg, the grated zest of 1 lemon and 1 tablespoon chopped parsley. Season and pour over the vegetables.
5 Sprinkle 50 g / 2 oz grated Gruyère cheese over the top and bake for 30–35 minutes until golden. Serve immediately.

Leek, Ham and Camembert Grill

Camembert melts really well for this dish, but other types of cheese work too. If you don't have Camembert, use crumbled Stilton, grated Gruyère or even mature Cheddar instead – they add their own distinctive flavour.

PREPARATION: 20 MINUTES
COOKING: ABOUT 25 MINUTES
SERVES 4
600 ml / 1 pint chicken or vegetable stock
700 g / 1 lb 9 oz scrubbed unpeeled potatoes, thickly sliced
450 g / 1 lb leeks (about 2 medium), sliced
100 g / 4 oz wafer-thin slices of ham
salt and pepper
125 g / 4^1/$_2$ oz Camembert cheese, thinly sliced
broccoli or green beans, to serve

1 In a large pan, heat the stock to boiling, then add the potatoes. Cook for 15 minutes until just tender, adding the leeks for the last 5 minutes of cooking time. Drain, reserving 4 tablespoons of the stock.
2 Preheat the grill. Layer up the sliced potatoes and leeks with the ham in a shallow heatproof dish and season with salt and pepper between the layers. Pour over the reserved stock.
3 Lay the cheese on top, then grill for 5 minutes until the cheese has melted and is beginning to brown.
4 Serve immediately with broccoli or green beans.

VARIATIONS: For a more luxurious gratin, pour 200 ml / 7 fl oz crème fraîche over the layers instead of the stock. You can also add a crushed garlic clove or two to the crème fraîche if you like. If you prefer you can also bake the dish in an oven preheated to 180°C / 350°F / gas 4 for about 20-25 minutes.

Carrot and Potato Flat Bread

PREPARATION: 15 MINUTES
COOKING: ABOUT 50 MINUTES
SERVES 12
butter, for greasing
450 g / 1 lb new potatoes, scrubbed
1 medium egg
300 ml / ^{1}/$_2$ pint semi-skimmed milk
2 tbsp chopped fresh rosemary
3 small carrots, grated
100 g / 3^1/$_2$ oz rice flour
100 g / 3^1/$_2$ oz potato flour
25 g / 1 oz soya flour
1 tsp bicarbonate of soda
^{1}/$_2$ tsp cream of tartar
salt and pepper
^{1}/$_2$ tsp rock salt

1 Preheat the oven to 220°C / 425°F / gas 7. Grease a 20 × 30 cm / 8 × 12 inch baking tin and line it with greaseproof paper. Cook the potatoes in boiling salted water for 8–10 minutes until tender. Drain, allow to cool and then slice.
2 Beat the egg and milk together. Stir half the rosemary into the egg mixture and add the grated carrot.
3 In a separate bowl, combine the dry ingredients except the remaining rosemary and rock salt. Fold into the egg mixture. Season to taste.
4 Pour the mixture into the prepared tin. Arrange the sliced potatoes on top and sprinkle with the remaining rosemary and the rock salt.
5 Bake for 35–40 minutes, until a skewer inserted into the bread comes out clean.

Polenta, Red Pepper and Courgette Gratin

If you've never used polenta, you'll be surprised how easy it is to cook with, and how well it complements the flavour of the grilled vegetables.

PREPARATION: 35 MINUTES
COOKING: 30–45 MINUTES
SERVES 4

15 g / $^1/_2$ oz butter, plus more for greasing
2 medium red peppers
3 tbsp olive oil
2 aubergines, thickly sliced
2 large courgettes, sliced lengthwise
2 garlic cloves, finely chopped
150 g / 5$^1/_2$ oz mozzarella cheese, sliced
600 ml / 1 pint vegetable stock
100 g / 4 oz quick-cook polenta
100 g / 4 oz Gruyère cheese, grated
2 tbsp chopped fresh thyme, or 2 tsp dried
salt and pepper

1 Preheat the oven to 200°C / 400°F / gas 6 and preheat the grill to high. Butter a 1.4 litre / 2$^1/_2$ pint shallow ovenproof dish. Place the peppers under the grill and cook for 5–7 minutes, turning occasionally, until blackened all over. Seal in a plastic bag and set aside to cool.
2 Brush oil over the aubergine and courgette slices, then grill for 3–4 minutes on each side until lightly browned. When the peppers are cool, halve them, remove the skin, core and seeds. Slice the flesh. Place all the vegetables in the prepared dish, scatter over the garlic and top with the mozzarella.
3 In a large pan, bring the stock to the boil. Add the polenta in a steady stream and cook for 3–4 minutes, stirring constantly, until thickened and starting to come away from the sides of the pan.
4 Off the heat, stir in half the Gruyère, the 15 g / $^1/_2$ oz butter and the thyme, then season well. Spoon the polenta over the mozzarella. Sprinkle over the remaining Gruyère and bake for 20–30 minutes until the top has a rich, golden colour.

Tian of Courgettes

This dish is a favourite with everyone as it is very filling.
It can also be served cold with salads and is ideal for picnics.

PREPARATION: 20 MINUTES

COOKING: 1 HOUR

SERVES 8

25 g / 1 oz butter, plus more for greasing

4 tbsp olive oil

500 g / 1 lb 2 oz leeks, trimmed and chopped

3 garlic cloves, finely chopped

1 kg / 2^1/$_4$ lb courgettes, trimmed and diced

500 g / 1 lb 2 oz frozen spinach, defrosted and drained

140 g / 5 oz brown rice, cooked according to packet instructions

5 large eggs, beaten

250 g / 9 oz Gruyère cheese, grated

salt and pepper

50 g / 2 oz Parmesan cheese, grated

50 g / 2 oz fresh breadcrumbs

1 Preheat the oven to 180°C / 350°F / gas 4. Lightly butter the base and sides of a shallow 1.5 litre / 2^3/$_4$ pint ovenproof gratin dish.

2 Heat the oil in a large pan, add the leeks and cook over a low heat for 5–6 minutes, stirring occasionally, until softened. Add the garlic and courgettes and cook for a further 10 minutes until tender, turning the vegetables over occasionally.

3 Remove the vegetables from the heat and stir in the spinach, cooked rice, eggs and Gruyère, mixing well to combine. Season generously. Spread the mixture into the prepared dish and sprinkle the Parmesan and breadcrumbs evenly over the top.

4 Dot with the 25 g / 1 oz butter and bake for 45 minutes, until the top is golden and the mixture is lightly set.

Polenta Squash Layer

PREPARATION: 20 MINUTES

COOKING: 1 HOUR

SERVES 4

700 ml / 1^1/$_4$ pints vegetable stock

225 g / 8 oz quick-cook polenta

75 g / 3 oz Parmesan cheese, grated

100 g / 4 oz butter

salt and pepper

1 small butternut squash (about 500 g / 1 lb 2 oz), peeled, deseeded and chopped

1 small onion, chopped

2 garlic cloves, crushed

100 g / 4 oz button mushrooms, sliced

140 g / 5 oz spinach, stalks removed

2 fresh sage leaves, chopped

175 g / 6 oz ricotta cheese

1 Line a 27 × 40 cm / 10^3/$_4$ × 16 inch baking tin with plastic film. Put the stock in a large pan and bring to a rolling boil. Shower in the polenta and cook, stirring constantly, for 3–4 minutes until thickened and coming away from the sides. Off the heat, beat in half the Parmesan and half the butter until smooth. Season and spoon into the prepared tin, spreading the surface to ensure it goes into all the corners. Allow to cool.

2 Preheat the oven to 190°C / 375°F / gas 5. Cook the butternut squash in a pan of lightly salted boiling water for 6–8 minutes until tender. Drain.

3 Meanwhile, heat the remaining butter in a large pan and fry the onion and garlic for 3–4 minutes, stirring occasionally, until softened slightly. Stir in the mushrooms and cook for 10 minutes, stirring occasionally. Stir in the spinach, cover and simmer for 2 minutes. Stir in the squash, sage and seasoning to taste.

4 Cut the polenta into 12 rectangles. Spread the ricotta cheese over 8 of these rectangles and season. Place 4 of these rectangles, cheese-side up, on a lightly oiled baking tray and spread them with half the mushroom mixture, then top each with another cheese-topped rectangle and more mushroom mixture. Top with a plain piece of polenta. Sprinkle over the remaining Parmesan and bake for 35–40 minutes until golden.

Creamy Mushroom Lasagne

This recipe uses chestnut and field mushrooms, but this is a versatile dish and you could use any combination of mushrooms that take your fancy.

PREPARATION: 25 MINUTES
COOKING: 35–40 MINUTES
SERVES 4

25 g / 1 oz butter

600 g / 1 lb 5 oz mixed mushrooms, such as
   chestnut and field, thinly sliced

2 garlic cloves, crushed

250 g / 9 oz fresh lasagne sheets

142 ml / $\frac{1}{2}$ pint carton of double cream

grated zest of 1 lemon

250 g / 9 oz ricotta or curd cheese

salt and pepper

oil, for greasing

4 tbsp chopped fresh parsley

300 g / 10 oz mozzarella, drained and
   thinly sliced

4 tbsp freshly grated Parmesan cheese

1 Preheat the oven to 220°C / 425°F / gas 7. Melt the butter in a large frying pan and gently cook the sliced mushrooms and crushed garlic for 5–8 minutes until softened.

2 Put the pasta into a large bowl and cover with boiling water; set aside for 5 minutes.

3 Pour the cream into a small pan and heat gently. Stir in the lemon zest and simmer gently for 2–3 minutes. Carefully stir in the ricotta or curd cheese. Gently heat through and season well.

4 Drain the pasta well. In an oiled ovenproof dish, layer the lasagne, ricotta mixture, garlic mushrooms, parsley, mozzarella and Parmesan. Continue these layers, finishing with the lasagne, a little sauce, some mozzarella and a sprinkling of Parmesan. (If you like, the dish can be prepared ahead up to this point and then chilled overnight).

5 Bake for 30 minutes, until the pasta is tender and the top is bubbling and well browned.

Vegetable Lasagne

This recipe may look long and complicated, but it isn't. This is one of those curious dishes that is much more difficult to explain than it is actually to do.

PREPARATION: 50 MINUTES
COOKING: 35–40 MINUTES
SERVES 6
1 aubergine
3 medium courgettes
3 tbsp olive oil
salt and pepper
3 peppers (red or yellow)
225 g / 8 oz lasagne sheets
4 tbsp chopped fresh parsley
50 g / 2 oz Parmesan cheese, grated
175 g / 6 oz mozzarella cheese,
    thinly sliced
FOR THE TOMATO SAUCE:
2 tbsp olive oil
1 onion, finely chopped
2 garlic cloves, crushed
1 carrot, grated
two 400 g / 14 oz cans of chopped
    tomatoes
150 ml / ¼ pint red wine (optional)
handful of fresh basil leaves
FOR THE BECHAMEL SAUCE:
50 g / 2 oz butter
40 g / 1½ oz plain flour
600 ml / 1 pint semi-skimmed milk
pinch of freshly grated nutmeg

1 First make the tomato sauce: heat the oil in a large heavy-based pan and cook the onion and garlic for 3 minutes until softened. Stir in the carrot and cook for a further 2 minutes. Add the tomatoes and wine and season to taste. Simmer for 25–30 minutes until the sauce is thickened and reduced. Stir in the basil and set aside.

2 Preheat the oven to 220°C / 425°F / gas 7. Cut the aubergine and courgettes lengthwise into 5 mm / ¼ inch thick slices. Brush with some olive oil, sprinkle on a little salt and place on a baking sheet. Bake for 15–20 minutes until browned and softened. At the same time, bake the peppers whole for 15–20 minutes until the skin is slightly charred and wrinkled. After removing them from the oven, place the peppers in a plastic bag until completely cool, then halve them, remove skin and seeds and cut the flesh into wide strips.

3 Make the béchamel sauce: melt the butter in a medium-sized heavy-based saucepan. Stir in the flour and cook, stirring, over a gentle heat. Remove from the heat and gradually pour in the milk, stirring constantly with a balloon whisk or wooden spoon. Return to the heat and continue whisking for about 5 minutes until the sauce thickens. Stir in the nutmeg and season well. Remove from the heat and set aside.

4 To assemble the lasagne, spoon half of the tomato sauce into the bottom of a 20 × 25 cm / 8 × 10 inch lasagne dish. Arrange one-third of the lasagne sheets in a single layer on top.

5 Cover the lasagne with half of the aubergines and sprinkle with a little parsley, then add half the peppers and courgettes. Spoon a third of the béchamel on top and sprinkle with a third of the Parmesan and mozzarella.

6 Repeat with another third of the lasagne, the remaining tomato sauce and vegetables and another third of the béchamel sauce and cheeses. Finally, top with the remaining pasta, béchamel and cheeses.

7 Cover with foil and bake for 25–30 minutes, then remove the foil and bake for 10 minutes until browned and bubbling.

The cabbage is one of the most ancient of cultivated vegetables dating back over 4,000 years. The Celts are reckoned to have brought it to Europe from Asia and there its ability to thrive in cold climates made it one of the most popular of crops.

Cabbage can be fabulous or foul, depending on how it is cooked. Properly cooked it retains its crunch, flavour and copious nutrients; overcooked and it loses them all, as well as producing the depressingly pervasive sulphurous odour so redolent of institutional cooking. When boiling cabbage, to keep the crispness and colour, cook for just 5–7 minutes.

Look for cabbages with firm but tender unblemished leaves that are neither withered nor puffy; the denser-hearted winter varieties like the Savoy and red cabbages should be firm and solid in their centres and weigh heavy for their size. Try to buy them with their loose outer leaves still in place as these are good indicators of freshness and also help protect the inner leaves.

Don't forget that raw cabbage makes the ideal winter substitute for lettuce in salads. Shred it finely and dress it with mustardy or nutty vinaigrettes.

Cabbage

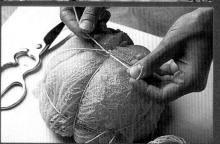

Sausage-stuffed Cabbage

1 Preheat the oven to 160°C / 325°F / gas 3. Bring a large pan of salted water to the boil. Pull any coarse leaves off the outside of a Savoy cabbage and trim the base so it stands straight. Carve out the centre of the stem from below – the hard woody bit – but keep it intact.

2 Plunge the cabbage into the pan of boiling water and boil for precisely 5 minutes. Drain and set aside to cool. Meanwhile, mix 450 g / 1 lb best-quality sausage meat, 1 beaten egg and some seasoning in a bowl.

3 When the cabbage is cool enough to handle, slowly peel back all the leaves like a flower. Stop when you get to the tiny leaves in the centre.

4 Put a tablespoon of the sausage meat at the base of the last leaf you pulled back. Continue, gradually reassembling the cabbage and holding it in shape as you do. Keep the filling to the base of each leaf – it shouldn't squeeze out.

5 Tie the cabbage into shape. Put a length of string around the middle and tie in place, then tie other lengths around the cabbage at intervals until it feels secure.

6 Put in a large lidded pot with 600 ml / 1 pint gravy or chicken stock and white wine, and cover with a little lightly buttered foil. Put on the lid and bake for 3–4 hours, or until meltingly tender.

7 Remove the string and slice the stuffed cabbage as you would a cake.

Cabbage Parcels with Roasted Ratatouille

PREPARATION: 25 MINUTES

COOKING: 40 MINUTES

SERVES 4

2 onions, cut into wedges

2 large aubergines, roughly chopped

8 tomatoes, quartered

4 tbsp olive oil

175 g / 6 oz long-grain rice

8 thin Lincolnshire or other herby sausages

2 red peppers, deseeded, cored and chopped

2 tbsp chopped fresh parsley

175 g / 6 oz mature Cheddar cheese, grated

salt and freshly ground black pepper

8 Savoy cabbage lettuce leaves, thick veins
   removed

1 Preheat the oven to 190°C / 375°F / gas 5.
Put the onions, aubergines and tomatoes
in a roasting tin, drizzle with oil and
season. Bake for 30 minutes until the
vegetables start to brown.

2 Cook the rice in boiling salted water
until tender, then drain. Fry the sausages
in a non-stick pan for 8– 10 minutes,
turning occasionally, until brown and
cooked; remove from the pan. Add the
peppers to the pan and cook for 4–5
minutes, stirring occasionally, until
softened. Chop the sausages and stir
into the pan with the parsley, rice and
cheese, then season.

3 Blanch the cabbage leaves in boiling
salted water for 2 minutes. Drain and
pat dry. Spoon some rice into the
centre of each leaf; roll up and tuck in
the ends.

4 Sit the parcels on the vegetables, joins
down. Heat in the oven for 10 minutes.
Cut each parcel in half before serving.

Roast Filled Onions

PREPARATION: 15 MINUTES

COOKING: 1 HOUR 20 MINUTES

SERVES 4

4 large onions, sliced into quarters but
the root left intact

2 tbsp olive oil

salt and pepper

2 large potatoes, grated

2 large carrots, grated

3 tbsp wholegrain mustard

25 g / 1 oz butter

85 g / 3 oz Gruyère cheese, grated

1 Preheat the oven to 200°C / 400°F / gas 6. Place the onions on a baking tray, brush with the olive oil, season and bake for about 1 hour until golden and tender.

2 Meanwhile, mix the potato and carrot together and stir in the mustard and seasoning. Divide the mixture between the onions and dot the top of each with the butter.

3 Return the onions to the oven and bake for 15 minutes more, until they are meltingly tender.

4 Sprinkle with the Gruyère cheese and cook for a further 5 minutes, until the topping is golden and bubbling.

Roast Squash with Lime and Caper Sauce

Deep-fried capers are a revelation – nutty, crisp and capery all in one. Sizzle them up in a little oil at the last minute to get them at their best. Serve this dish from Sophie Grigson as a light lunch, or as an accompaniment to grilled meat.

PREPARATION: 20 MINUTES

COOKING: 40 MINUTES

SERVES 4

1 kabocha or onion squash, or wedge of
pumpkin, about 900 g–1.3 kg / 2–3 lb

6 garlic cloves, unpeeled

2 tbsp sunflower oil or light olive oil

2 sprigs of thyme or lemon thyme

2 bay leaves

1 sprig of rosemary

FOR THE LIME AND CAPER SAUCE:

140 g / 5 oz pot of natural yoghurt

juice of 1 lime

1 heaped tbsp large capers (rinsed and
soaked if salted), chopped

FOR THE FRIED CAPERS:

sunflower oil

2 heaped tbsp capers (rinsed and soaked
if salted), dried thoroughly

1 Preheat the oven to 200°C / 400°F / gas 6. Cut the squash into 2.5–4 cm / 1–1½ inch wedges (discard the seeds, but leave the skin on). Put in a roasting tin with the garlic, oil and herbs; coat the squash and garlic in the oil. Roast for 40 minutes, turning once or twice, until the squash is tender.

2 Make the Lime and Caper Sauce by mixing together all the ingredients.

3 Fry the capers: heat enough sunflower oil to fill a small pan to a depth of about 1 cm / ½ inch until a bread cube browns in it in 20 seconds. Test a couple of capers by frying them for 10 seconds if small, 15 seconds if large. Lift out and drain on kitchen paper; they should be crisp and retain some colour. If black or bitter, reduce the heat and try again.

4 Divide the squash between four plates or bowls. Drizzle with a little sauce and scatter with fried capers. Serve the rest of the sauce in a jug.

Make it Mediterranean

The Mediterranean diet has always made the most of an abundance of sun-ripened vegetables, enhanced by the warmth of Mediterranean flavourings like olives and olive oil, garlic, pine nuts, basil and oregano. They are used to make a diverse range of pasta dressings, in glorious multicoloured toppings for pizzas and in the most tempting of creamy risottos.

Pasta, Pizza, Risotto, etc

Pasta with Broccoli and Toasted Nuts

Instead of Camembert, try crumbling in some blue cheese or feta, or simply shave some Parmesan over the top.

PREPARATION: 15 MINUTES
COOKING: 15–20 MINUTES
SERVES 2 (EASILY DOUBLED)
175 g / 6 oz spaghetti
salt and pepper
200 g / 8 oz broccoli, cut into small florets
olive oil, for frying and dressing
50 g / 2 oz mixed chopped nuts
1 garlic clove, finely chopped
3 tbsp chopped fresh parsley
grated zest and juice of 1 small lemon
115 g / 4 oz Camembert or Brie, cut into
    small pieces

1 Cook the pasta in lots of rapidly boiling salted water until just tender. Add the broccoli for the last 3 minutes of cooking time.
2 Heat a little olive oil in a small pan, add the nuts and cook until lightly toasted, stirring frequently. Add the garlic and cook for about 20 seconds until just brown. Remove from the heat and stir in the parsley and lemon zest.
3 Drain the pasta and broccoli, then return them to the pan and stir in the nut mixture and cheese.
4 Season, then drizzle with some olive oil and lemon juice to serve.

Cheesy Spaghetti with Courgettes and Bacon

This simple, easy-to-do pasta bake is a great way of getting children to eat their greens – and tastes really delicious too.

PREPARATION: 20 MINUTES
COOKING: 20–25 MINUTES
SERVES 4
350 g / 12 oz spaghetti
salt and pepper
25 g / 1 oz butter, plus more for the dish
1 onion, finely chopped
8 slices of smoked streaky bacon, rind
    removed and cut into small strips
25 g / 1 oz plain flour
600 ml / 1 pint milk
200 g / 8 oz courgettes, cut into
    matchstick strips
200 g / 8 oz mature Cheddar cheese,
    finely grated
2 rounded tbsp whole-grain mustard

1 Preheat the oven to 220°C / 425°F / gas 7. Cook the spaghetti in lots of rapidly boiling salted water until just al dente.
2 Meanwhile, melt the butter in a pan and cook the onion and bacon for 5 minutes until softened and golden. Sprinkle over the flour and cook for 1 minute, stirring gently. Gradually add the milk, stirring to make a thick smooth sauce.
3 Bring the sauce to the boil, add the courgettes and simmer for a couple of minutes. Remove from the heat and stir in all but a handful of the cheese and all the mustard. Season.
4 Drain the pasta well and mix with the cheese sauce. Spoon the mixture into a large buttered ovenproof dish and scatter over the reserved cheese. Bake for 20–25 minutes until bubbling and golden brown.

Spaghetti alla Puttanesca

The name of this famous Italian dish translates literally as 'whore's spaghetti'. This recipe is Sophie Grigson's version.

PREPARATION: 10–15 MINUTES

COOKING: 10–12 MINUTES

SERVES 3–4

400 g / 14 oz dried spaghetti

salt and pepper

4 tbsp olive oil

400 g / 14 oz can of chopped tomatoes

1 red chilli, deseeded and finely chopped

8 canned anchovy fillets, drained and chopped

2 garlic cloves, chopped

25 g / 1 oz butter

100 g / 4 oz stoned black olives, sliced

2 tbsp small capers (rinsed and soaked if salted)

4 tbsp chopped parsley

1 Cook the pasta in lots of rapidly boiling salted water.

2 Heat 1 tablespoon of the oil in a pan. Add the tomatoes. Bring to the boil and cook for 4–5 minutes, stirring and crushing them with a wooden spoon.

3 Fry the chilli, anchovies and garlic in the remaining oil and the butter for 1–2 minutes, mashing the anchovies.

4 Add the tomatoes, olives and capers. Cook for 2–3 minutes, stirring.

5 Drain the pasta when it is just al dente. Add to the sauce. Sprinkle over the parsley and some seasoning. Stir well before serving.

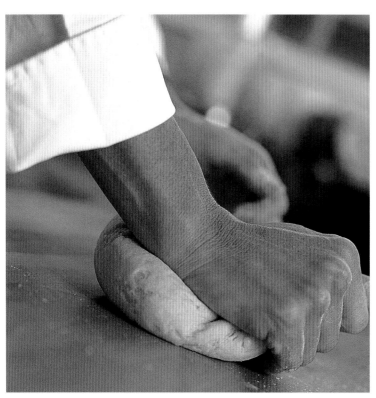

Fennel Raviolini

Home-made pasta is easier than you think, as Ursula Ferrigno demonstrates here. For the best results use '00' flour, a very fine-textured wheat flour traditionally used in Italy; it is available from large supermarkets and delicatessens. If you can't find it, use strong plain bread flour instead. Semolina flour helps the pasta to dry. It also helps give the recipe an authentic Italian flavour, as well as its wonderful yellow colour.

PREPARATION: 40 MINUTES,
PLUS CHILLING AND
RESTING
SERVES 6

FOR THE PASTA:
100 g / 4 oz '00' flour
100 g / 4 oz grano duro di semolo
   (semolina flour)
2 large eggs
2 tsp fine sea salt
1 tbsp extra-virgin olive oil

1 First make the pasta: open all the windows to cool the kitchen and rinse your hands in cold water. Sift the flours into a mound on a clean work surface and make a well in the centre. Break in the eggs and add the salt and olive oil. Beat the eggs lightly with a fork and draw in the flour without allowing the egg to escape, until you have a rough-textured dough.

2 Use your hands to bring the rough dough into a smooth ball. Discard any crusty flour and knead the dough on the work surface, adding a little more '00' flour if necessary, for 8–10 minutes until the dough is silky smooth. Wrap in plastic film and chill for 20 minutes.

3 Meanwhile, make the filling. Lightly steam the chopped fennel for 5 minutes over a pan of simmering water. Allow to cool slightly, then beat

FOR THE FILLING:

1 small fennel bulb, finely chopped

200 g / 8 oz ricotta cheese

15 g / ½ oz pack of fresh basil leaves, shredded

50 g / 2 oz Parmesan cheese, grated, plus extra shavings to serve

with the ricotta cheese, fresh basil and freshly grated Parmesan. Season to taste.

4 Remove the dough from the fridge – it should now be smooth and marbled. Cut off one-eighth of the dough, wrap the rest in plastic film and return it to the fridge. Roll out the piece of dough on a lightly floured surface to flatten it slightly – it should measure about 20 × 7 cm / 8 × 2¾ inches.

5 Adjust the pasta machine to the thickest setting. Sprinkle semolina flour over the rollers to stop the dough sticking. Roll dough through the machine. Repeat, then move machine on to the next setting and roll dough through in a continuous motion, twice. Repeat until you reach the second thinnest setting. (Many experts never put the pasta through on the final setting as they find it often tears.) Lay the strip on a work surface and leave to rest for 8–10 minutes. Repeat with the remaining dough.

6 Use a 7.5 cm / 3 inch fluted cutter to cut out about 54 pasta circles. Spoon three-quarters of a teaspoon of the filling into the centre of each circle of dough. Brush the edges with a little water, fold each circle over in half and pinch the edges together to seal.

7 Arrange the finished raviolini on a wire rack and leave to dry for at least 15 minutes. (If you aren't going to use the pasta straight away transfer to the freezer at this stage – it can be frozen for up to 3 months.) Keep the leftover dough and cut into small pieces and dry with the rest of the pasta. These can then be added to soup as a thickener.

Fennel Raviolini with Roasted Vegetable and Saffron Sauce

Here Ursula Ferrigno dresses her raviolini with a delicious sauce of roasted fennel and onions delicately flavoured with saffron.

PREPARATION: 15 MINUTES
COOKING: 25 MINUTES
SERVES 6
fennel raviolini, as previous pages
2 fennel bulbs, trimmed and sliced
4 small red onions, cut into wedges
5 tbsp extra-virgin olive oil
salt and pepper
1 garlic clove, finely chopped
2 shallots, finely chopped
large pinch of saffron threads
250 ml / 9 fl oz dry white wine
350 g / 12 oz mascarpone cheese
fresh basil and flat-leaf parsley, to serve

1 To prepare the roasted vegetables and saffron sauce: preheat the oven to 190°C / 375°F / gas 5. Place the fennel and onions on a large baking tray and drizzle over 4 table-spoons of the olive oil. Season and roast for 25 minutes until just beginning to char.

2 Meanwhile, heat the remaining olive oil in a pan and sweat the garlic and shallots for 5 minutes over a low heat until softened. Stir in the saffron and wine, bring to the boil and simmer until reduced by half.

3 Stir in the mascarpone cheese and beat the mixture until smooth. Cook over a low heat, stirring, for 5 minutes. The more you cook the sauce, the more yellow it will become, as the saffron gradually infuses into the mixture.

4 Bring a large pan of slightly salted water to the boil and add the raviolini. Return to the boil and cook for 3–4 minutes (frozen pasta will take 5–6 minutes). Drain and toss with the roasted vegetables and saffron sauce. Serve sprinkled with the Parmesan shavings and fresh herbs.

Fiorelli with Oven-dried Vegetables and Tapenade

PREPARATION: 15 MINUTES
COOKING: 1 HOUR
SERVES 4
2–3 courgettes, cut into thickish slices at an angle
225 g / 8 oz tasty cherry tomatoes, such as Santa, halved and pulp and seeds removed
salt and pepper
1 tbsp caster sugar
2 tbsp olive oil
350 g / 12 oz dried fiorelli (pasta trumpets)
mixed fresh herbs, to garnish (optional)
freshly grated Parmesan cheese, to serve
FOR THE TAPENADE:
225 g / 8 oz stoned black olives
1 tbsp capers, drained
1 fat garlic clove
1 tsp lemon juice
5 tbsp extra-virgin olive oil

1 To prepare the oven-dried vegetables: preheat the oven to 150°C / 300°F / gas 2. Place the courgette slices and tomato halves on a large baking tray and sprinkle with a little salt and caster sugar, then drizzle over the olive oil. Put in the oven for about 1 hour, turning the tray from time to time so the vegetables receive even heat.

2 Meanwhile, make the tapenade: put the olives, capers, garlic, lemon juice and olive oil in a food processor and whizz to a paste.

3 Bring a large pan of salted water to the boil and add the pasta. Bring back to a good rolling boil and cook until just al dente (probably 5–6 minutes). Drain.

4 Stir the tapenade into the pasta and toss with the oven-dried vegetables. Garnish with herbs if you like and serve with the Parmesan.

Grilled Vegetable Pasticcio

PREPARATION: 50 MINUTES
COOKING: 30 MINUTES
SERVES 8

3 red and 3 yellow peppers, deseeded and quartered
2 large aubergines, thinly sliced lengthwise
3 tbsp olive oil
500 g / 1 lb tagliatelle
25 g / 1 oz butter
1 small onion, very finely chopped
2 garlic cloves, crushed
6 tbsp white wine or dry vermouth
284 ml / $\frac{1}{2}$ pint carton of double cream
225 g / 8 oz Gruyère cheese, finely grated
salt and pepper
2 eggs, lightly beaten

1 Preheat the grill to high and oven to 190°C / 375°F / gas 5. Grill the peppers, skin-side up, for 5–6 minutes until the skin is blackened and blistered. Place in a plastic bag and leave to steam for about 5 minutes, so the skins will loosen.
2 Brush both sides of the aubergine slices with the olive oil and season. Heat a griddle pan and fry the aubergine slices for 2–3 minutes on each side until scorched. Use to line a deep 23 cm / 9 inch loose-bottomed tin, overlapping the slices and allowing them to overhang the edges of the tin.
3 Cook the pasta until just tender. Meanwhile, melt the butter in a small pan and fry the onion and garlic for 2–3 minutes until softened. Stir in wine or vermouth and cream and heat gently until almost boiling. Remove from the heat and stir in the cheese. Season, allow to cool slightly and stir in the eggs.
4 Drain the pasta, return to the pan and mix in the sauce.
5 Peel the peppers. Spoon half the pasta into the aubergine-lined tin and level. Cover with the red peppers. Spoon over the remaining pasta and top with the yellow peppers. Fold the overhanging aubergine slices in over the filling.
6 Cover with buttered greaseproof paper and bake for 30 minutes until firm. Allow to stand for a few minutes before turning out on a plate.

Spicy Pepper Penne

Chorizo gives this pasta dish a delightful spicy kick, but you could use the same quantity of thinly sliced salami if you prefer.

PREPARATION: 15 MINUTES
COOKING: 25–30 MINUTES
SERVES 4

4 tbsp olive oil
3 red peppers, deseeded, cored and cut into 1 cm / $\frac{1}{2}$ inch wide strips
1 large onion, thinly sliced
2 garlic cloves, crushed
two 400 g / 14 oz cans of chopped tomatoes
salt and pepper
300 g / 10 oz penne or rigatoni
140 g / 5 oz sliced chorizo
butter, for greasing
1 slice of white bread, made into crumbs
2 tbsp chopped fresh rosemary or 2 tsp dried
25 g / 1 oz freshly grated Parmesan cheese

1 Preheat the oven to 200°C / 400°F / gas 6. Heat 3 tablespoons of the oil in a pan and cook the peppers and onion for 10 minutes until soft and golden, shaking the pan occasionally. Stir in the garlic and cook for 1 minute. Add the tomatoes and heat through. Season.
2 Meanwhile, cook the pasta in lots of rapidly boiling salted water until just al dente. Drain well and mix it with the sauce and chorizo. Spoon the mixture into a buttered large shallow ovenproof dish.
3 Mix together the breadcrumbs, rosemary and Parmesan, then sprinkle over the pasta. (You can make ahead up to this point and chill overnight.)
4 Drizzle with remaining oil and bake for 15–20 minutes until golden.

Marinated Couscous with Harissa Tomatoes

Harissa, a Moroccan chilli paste, is available from better super-markets and food shops. If you can't find any, just mix some chilli sauce into 2 teaspoons tomato purée and use that instead.

PREPARATION: 10 MINUTES

COOKING: 15 MINUTES

SERVES 4

250 g / 9 oz ready-cooked couscous

350 ml / 12 fl oz vegetable stock

4 sun-dried tomatoes in oil, drained and chopped

50 g / 2 oz stoned olives, quartered

1 tbsp capers

25 g / 1 oz fresh coriander, chopped

salt and pepper

FOR THE HARISSA TOMATOES:

1 tbsp olive oil

2 tsp harissa (see above)

6 plum tomatoes, halved

40 g / 1¹/₂ oz rocket

1 Place the couscous in a shallow dish and pour the stock over it. Leave to stand for 10 minutes until all the stock has been absorbed.

2 Meanwhile, make the harissa tomatoes: brush a large griddle pan with 1 teaspoon of the oil and heat until smoking-hot. Mix the remaining oil with the harissa and spread over the cut sides of the tomatoes. Place, cut-side down, on the griddle pan and cook for 2 minutes.

3 Fluff the couscous up with a fork. Stir the sun-dried tomatoes, olives, capers and coriander into the couscous and season.

4 Divide the couscous between 4 serving plates. Arrange the tomatoes over the couscous, top with the rocket and serve.

Tomato and Mushroom Stacks

Ready-made polenta is sold in large sausage or oblong shapes and is not to be confused with quick-cook polenta, still in grain form.

PREPARATION: 20 MINUTES
COOKING: ABOUT 30 MINUTES
SERVES 4
500 g / 1 lb 2 oz ready-made polenta (see above)
$^1/_2$ tsp dried oregano
25 g / 1 oz freshly grated Parmesan cheese
50 g / 2 oz Cheddar cheese, grated
4 tbsp olive oil
salt and pepper
4 large flat mushrooms, stalks removed
400 g / 14 oz tomatoes, roughly chopped
1 garlic clove, finely chopped

1 Preheat the oven to 220°C / 425°F / gas 7. Cut the polenta into 12 slices about 1 cm / $^1/_2$ inch thick and stack these in 4 overlapping piles. Sprinkle with oregano and most of the cheeses.
2 Pour the oil into a bowl, season and brush each mushroom with it. Place stalk-side up on the polenta stacks.
3 Tip the tomatoes and garlic into the remaining oil. Spoon the tomatoes and their juices in and around the mushrooms and polenta, then season with salt and pepper. Sprinkle over the remaining cheese.
4 Roast in the oven for about 30 minutes, until the tomatoes have softened and the mushrooms are tender. Serve hot.

Mozzarella Pasta with Olives and Chilli

PREPARATION: 15 MINUTES
COOKING: ABOUT 15 MINUTES
SERVES 4
350 g / 12 oz penne or rigatoni
salt and pepper
1 small red onion, finely chopped
1 red chilli, deseeded and finely chopped
450 g / 1 lb ripe tomatoes, chopped
6 tbsp olive oil
200 g / 8 oz buffalo mozzarella, chopped
handful of small fresh basil or mint leaves
100 g / 4 oz black olives

1 Cook the pasta in a large pan of boiling salted water for 10–12 minutes until just *al dente*, stirring from time to time.
2 Meanwhile, in a large bowl, mix together the onion, chilli and tomatoes. Season with plenty of salt and pepper, then stir in the oil.
3 Drain the pasta and tip it into the tomato mixture, together with the mozzarella, basil and olives. Stir well and serve immediately.

VARIATION: This works best with authentic buffalo mozzarella; if you can't find that, however, rather than falling back on the bland blocks of cows'-milk substitute, try making the dish with another nice flavoursome melting cheese, like Fontina, or even Caerphilly.

Spinach is thought to have originated in Persia, where it was first cultivated for the delectation of their cats, and was brought to Europe by the Moors in the sixteenth century. It is therefore unusual among our common vegetables in having been unknown to the Ancient Romans. Catherine de Medici is credited with having introduced it to the French court, hence all dishes containing spinach being referred to by the French as *à la Florentine*.

Spinach can be quite gritty, so first soak the leaves for about an hour in cold water and then rinse them in several changes of fresh water, taking the leaves out to leave grit behind. The stalks and any tough ribs should also be removed. The best way to cook the leaves is in a tightly closed pan with just the water left clinging to them. Cooked spinach will absorb several times its own weight of melted butter and goes incredibly well with eggs and ham. Young leaves are also excellent raw in salads.

Although the leaves are highly nutritious, being notably rich in iron and vitamin A, the oxalic acid in spinach when cooked does not allow the abundance of nutrients to be absorbed by the body – so use the vegetable raw where you can.

Spinach

Roman Spinach

This simple treatment makes an excellent and characterful accompaniment to rich veal, poultry and fish dishes.

1 Cram 500 g / 1 lb cleaned and trimmed spinach leaves (see above) into a large pan. Cover and cook for 2–3 minutes, shaking occasionally, until the leaves are wilted. Drain in a colander.
2 Heat 2 tablespoons of olive oil in the rinsed-out pan and cook 3 tablespoons pine nuts for 1–2 minutes until just coloured.
3 Add 2 finely chopped garlic cloves and 1 deseeded and chopped red chilli. Cook for 1 minute more, until the nuts are golden.
4 Stir in 3 tablespoons of roughly chopped seedless raisins together with the drained spinach and cook for about 30 seconds or so.
5 Season well and serve.

Fennel Risotto

This recipe by Suzanna Gelmetti couldn't be simpler, or more authentic. The secret lies in using the right rice – arborio, carnaroli or vialone nano – and a good tasty stock.

PREPARATION: 15 MINUTES
COOKING: 35–40 MINUTES
SERVES 4 AS A MAIN COURSE OR 6 AS A STARTER
2 fennel bulbs
2 tbsp olive oil, plus more to serve
50 g / 2 oz butter
1 large onion, finely chopped
350 g / 12 oz risotto rice
150 ml / ¼ pint dry white wine
1.3 litre / 2¼ pints hot vegetable stock
50 g / 2 oz freshly grated Parmesan cheese, plus more to serve
salt and pepper

1 Core the fennel and dice; keep any fronds to garnish.
2 Heat the oil and half the butter in a large heavy-based pan. Cook the onion for 5 minutes until softened and golden. Add the rice and diced fennel, and cook for 5 minutes, stirring, until the rice is slightly translucent.
3 Turn up the heat and pour in the wine; let it bubble and simmer over a medium heat (this helps cook out the raw taste of the alcohol). When most of the wine has been absorbed, add a couple of ladlefuls of stock to cover the rice. Stir to prevent sticking; keep the rice on the boil. The grains will become plump and moist.
4 Cook over a moderate heat, stirring all the time, adding ladlefuls of stock to keep the consistency soupy. After 15 minutes, taste a grain; it should be creamy but with some bite. Don't worry if it seems a bit soupy, the rice will keep absorbing the liquid off the heat.
5 Add the remaining butter, cut in small pieces, and most of the Parmesan. Season and allow to stand for 1 minute before ladling on to plates or one large platter.
6 Scatter the risotto with a little more Parmesan, black pepper and oil. Serve immediately.

Leek and Blue Cheese Risotto

Just five ingredients can give you supper for four. Here the usual risotto procedure is simplified – all the stock is added in one go, so there is no need to stand and stir.

PREPARATION: 15 MINUTES
COOKING: 20–25 MINUTES
SERVES 4
2 large leeks
3 tbsp olive oil
300 g / 10 oz risotto rice
1 litre / 1¾ pints hot vegetable or chicken stock
175 g / 6 oz Stilton or Danish blue cheese, crumbled
salt and pepper

1 Trim the leeks and cut down the length to the centre. Wash under cold running water to remove any dirt, then slice thinly into rings.
2 Heat the oil in a heavy-based pan which has a lid. Add the leeks and fry quickly until bright green (about 2 minutes). Stir in the rice and cook for 2 minutes until the grains are glistening.
3 Meanwhile, in another pan, bring the stock to the boil.
4 Add the stock to the rice, stir and bring back to the boil. Cover and simmer without stirring for 12–15 minutes, until the rice is tender.
5 Remove from the heat and stir in the cheese and some pepper. Taste, season if necessary, stir and serve.

Chestnut Gnocchi with Sour Cranberries

This recipe from Paul Gayler makes a splendid vegetarian alternative on Christmas Day.

PREPARATION: 45 MINUTES, PLUS DRYING
COOKING: 45 MINUTES
SERVES 4

350 g / 12 oz floury potatoes (e.g., King Edward, Maris Piper)
75 g / 2³/₄ oz cooked chestnuts, finely ground
75 g / 2³/₄ oz Gruyère cheese, grated
15 g / ¹/₂ oz unsalted butter
2 medium egg yolks
125 g / 4¹/₂ oz plain flour
pinch of freshly grated nutmeg
FOR THE SAUCE:
225 ml / 8 fl oz vegetable stock
10 g / ¹/₃ oz dried wild mushrooms
50 g / 2 oz unsalted butter
2 shallots, finely chopped
1 garlic clove, crushed
100 g / 4 oz Jerusalem artichokes, peeled and sliced
1 tbsp balsamic vinegar
2 tbsp tamari (Japanese soy sauce)
150 g / 5¹/₂ oz cranberries
450 g / 1 lb small Brussels sprouts, trimmed and halved
salt and pepper
sprigs of fresh thyme, to garnish

1 Peel the potatoes and cook in a pan of lightly salted boiling water until tender. Drain well and mash. Add the ground chestnuts and Gruyère and beat well to allow the cheese to melt. Mix in the butter, egg yolks and half the flour. Add the nutmeg and season.

2 Turn the mixture out on a lightly floured surface and knead in the remaining flour, a little at a time, to form a smooth, soft dough. Leave to cool.

3 Roll out the gnocchi dough into long sausage shapes, each about 2.5 cm / 1 inch thick, and then cut them into 2 cm / ³/₄ inch lengths. Roll each piece over the prongs of a fork to form the classic ridged and slightly curved gnocchi shape. Place the gnocchi on a lightly floured baking tray and leave to dry for 1 hour.

4 Meanwhile, make the sauce: put the stock in a small pan and bring to the boil. Add the dried mushrooms, remove from the heat and leave to soak for about 1 hour. Strain the mushrooms, reserving the stock.

5 Heat a frying pan, add half the butter, the shallots, garlic, artichokes and soaked mushrooms and cook over a high heat for 5 minutes.

6 Pour in the reserved stock and cook for 10 minutes. Add the balsamic vinegar, tamari and cranberries and leave to simmer for a further 10 minutes.

7 Meanwhile, cook the Brussels sprouts in a large pan of lightly salted boiling water for 5–6 minutes. Remove with a slotted spoon and reserve.

8 Poach the gnocchi, in batches, in a large pan of lightly salted boiling water until they rise to the surface – this should take 2–3 minutes. Remove with a slotted spoon and drain well.

9 Melt the remaining butter in a frying pan and cook the Brussels sprouts and gnocchi over a gentle heat for 2 minutes, stirring occasionally. Season with more nutmeg and salt and pepper to taste.

10 Arrange the gnocchi in a serving dish, pour over the sauce and garnish with the sprigs of thyme.

The kneading begins in earnest. The dough will gradually lose its stickiness, so treat it as roughly as you like until you get the texture you need.

Pizza from Scratch

Pizzas come in two styles. The classic Neapolitan is thick and crunchy around the edge and thinner and softer in the middle. North of Rome, in big cities like Florence and Milan, they make the trendy pizza – paper-thin and with hardly any border. Here, in Suzanna Gelmetti's recipe, we are making Neapolitan.

Even if you like cooking with imperial measurements, this is the perfect recipe to cook in metric as the numbers are so easy. You can use strong white flour here, but far nicer – and now stocked by larger supermarkets and specialist delis – is the Italian type '00' which has the best flavour.

There is no more work in making three pizzas than in making one – in our photographs a triple quantity of dough is being made. Freeze the uncooked bases in their tins – defrost them before topping.

PREPARATION: 30 MINUTES, PLUS
2½ HOURS' PROVING
MAKES A PIZZA FOR 4–6 PEOPLE
250 ml / 9 fl oz water, warmed to blood heat
pinch of sugar
20 g / ¾ oz fresh yeast, or 1 sachet of
    easy-blend dried yeast

1 Put 3 tablespoons of the water and the sugar in a large bowl and stir in the fresh yeast (add easy-blend yeast to the flour, never to wet ingredients). Add 4 tablespoons of the flour and mix to a soft dough (add more flour or water if necessary). Knead for 3 minutes, sprinkle with flour, then cover with a tea towel and leave to rise for 30 minutes.
2 Gently rewarm the remaining water to blood heat. Tip the remaining flour on a work surface. Shape it into a volcano and put the starter dough

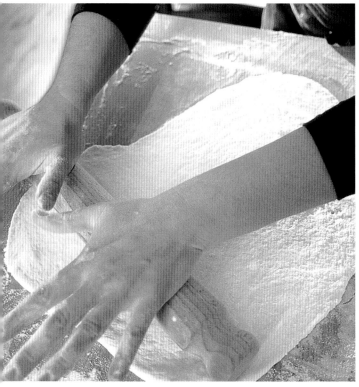

After a second rise, roll out the dough to fit your tin and press it firmly in, dimpling it as you do so.

500 g / 1 lb 2 oz Italian type 00 or strong white
  flour, plus more if necessary
3 tbsp extra-virgin olive oil, plus more for the
  baking tin
1 tbsp salt
for the toppings: see overleaf

in the crater. Pour over a little water and pinch dough, flour and water together to mix.
3 Gradually add more water, pinching together, until all the water is added, then repeat with the oil. When you have added a third of the oil and have a soft dough, make a dip in the top and add the salt and half the remaining oil.
4 Now knead everything together until it is no longer sticky and the work surface is clean. Toss the dough and stretch it into a flat shape, drizzle on half the remaining oil and knead, then repeat, kneading for a good minute more at the end. The dough is ready when it feels silky, but not too silky.
5 Put the dough back in the bowl and cut a cross in the top with a large sharp knife. Sprinkle with flour, cover with a tea towel and leave in a warm place to triple in size (about 2 hours).
6 Italians make round pizzas in pizzerias, but at home they're always rectangular – it is easier to fit in the oven! The ideal size for our recipes is a 30 × 40-cm / 12 × 16-inch baking tin with a shallow rim. Oil it with extra-virgin olive oil. Lightly flour your work surface and scoop the dough out on to it. Knead it or roll it for a few minutes, then press it evenly into the tin, leaving it heavily indented with your fingertips – it should be slightly thinner in the middle. Prick it all over with a fork. See overleaf for topping and baking.

Pizza Toppings

Now prepare your toppings as follows.
Preheat oven to 250°C / 475°F / gas 9 or
its highest setting. Add topping and bake
immediately for 18–20 minutes until
puffed and golden. Don't open the oven
for the first 15 minutes or you'll let the
heat out and your base won't be as crisp.

PIZZA CON MENTA ZUCCHINE
MINT AND COURGETTE PIZZA

Slice 3 courgettes at an angle and
quarter a garlic clove, then stir-fry in 3
tablespoons extra-virgin olive oil for 6–8
minutes. Allow to cool, then remove
garlic. Mix with 250 g / 9 oz chopped
mozzarella (preferably buffalo), a handful
of chopped mint and salt and pepper.
Spread over dough, sprinkle with extra-
virgin olive oil, salt and black pepper.

PIZZA NAPOLETANA

Drain 2 cans plum tomatoes and chop.
Deseed and chop a red chilli (optional).
Sprinkle over pizza and top with extra-
virgin olive oil, oregano and salt and
pepper. Drain a can of anchovy fillets
and crumble over the top. Sprinkle with
more oregano and olive oil.

PIZZA BIANCA CON SEMI DE
FINOCCHIO E FORMAGGIO
FENNEL SEED AND CHEESE PIZZA

Mix 4 heaped tablespoons each full-fat
soft cheese, ricotta and crème fraîche.
Season with black pepper and spread over
dough. Drizzle over some extra-virgin
olive oil, sprinkle with 3 tablespoons
fennel seeds and more pepper.

PIZZA AL FUNGHI E RICOTTA
MUSHROOM AND RICOTTA PIZZA

Break up 10 g / ⅓ oz porcini (dried ceps) and soak in warm water for 15 minutes, then drain. Drain 2 cans of plum tomatoes and chop roughly. Mix in a bowl with a little salt, 2 tablespoons of extra-virgin olive oil and a few roughly torn basil leaves. Slice 250 g / 9 oz mixed mushrooms (chestnut, chanterelle, oyster, or whatever you can get) and fry in 2 tablespoons extra-virgin olive oil with the dried mushrooms and a peeled quartered garlic clove for 6–8 minutes until browned and smelling nutty; remove garlic. Spread the tomato mixture over the dough, spoon over the mushrooms, then dot 225 g / 8 oz ricotta and some more shredded basil over the top.

PIZZA CON PORRI E PEPE NERO
LEEK AND BLACK PEPPER PIZZA

Sauté 3 thinly sliced leeks in 3 tablespoons extra-virgin olive oil and season. Spread dough with 200 g / 8 oz crème fraîche, spoon on leeks, Parmesan shavings, black pepper and more oil.

PIZZA CON RUCOLA
ROCKET PIZZA

Prick dough all over with a fork, brush with 4 tablespoons extra-virgin olive oil and sprinkle with sea salt. Bake blind for 15–18 minutes until golden, then cover with 600 g / 1 lb 5 oz cherry tomato quarters, a handful of torn rocket leaves and 250 g / 9 oz chopped mozzarella (preferably buffalo). Drizzle with some more extra-virgin olive oil.

Tomato and Oregano Pizza

This is a version of the classic Pizza Napoletana, without the anchovies.

PREPARATION: 5 MINUTES
COOKING: 15–20 MINUTES
MAKES ONE 30 CM/12 INCH PIZZA (SERVES 2–4)

1 beef tomato, sliced
1 prepared Pizza Base (see pages 108–9)
1 quantity Old-fashioned Tomato Sauce (see page 20)
8 yellow cherry tomatoes, halved
8 red cherry tomatoes, halved
1 garlic clove, thinly sliced
1 tbsp extra-virgin olive oil
salt and pepper
2 tsp fresh oregano leaves

1 Preheat the oven to 220°C / 425°F / gas 7. Layer the beef tomato slices over the pizza base. Spread the tomato sauce over them. Scatter over the cherry tomatoes and garlic. Drizzle with the oil and season with salt and black pepper.
2 Cook for 15–20 minutes, until golden at the edges and the tomatoes are slightly charred.
3 Scatter over the oregano just before serving.

Pimiento, Rocket and Mozzarella Pizza

The mozzarella cheese originally used for pizzas was traditionally made from the milk of water buffaloes. Today cows' milk is more commonly used, although the results are often more bland and rubbery than the authentic mozzarella di bufala. *You can't do better than home-made pesto, but for speed use a jar instead. Taste it first, as some brands can be a little salty.*

PREPARATION: 15 MINUTES
COOKING: 15–20 MINUTES
MAKES ONE 30 CM/12 INCH PIZZA (SERVES 2–4)

25 g / 1 oz fresh basil leaves
15 g / ^{1}/$_2$ oz Parmesan cheese, grated
1 garlic clove, halved
2 tsp pine nuts
3 tbsp olive oil
1 prepared Pizza Base (see pages 108–9)
400 g / 14 oz can of pimientos, drained and sliced
140 g / 5 oz mozzarella cheese, sliced
25 g / 1 oz rocket

1 Preheat the oven to 220°C / 425°F / gas 7. Place the basil, Parmesan, garlic and pine nuts in a food processor and process until coarsely chopped. With the motor still running, gradually add the oil to make a smooth paste.
2 Spread the pesto over the pizza base and arrange the sliced pimientos and mozzarella on top.
3 Cook for 15–20 minutes, until puffed and golden.
4 Scatter over the rocket and allow to wilt slightly before serving.

We take potatoes so much for granted we almost stop thinking of them as vegetables – and treat them like mere fillers. The humble potato is, however, as versatile as any leaf or stem, and can feature in dishes as diverse as delicate potato cakes for sophisticated starters, comforting flavoured mashes and that culinary miracle – the glorious chip.

Staple Diet

Ways with Potatoes

Full Meal Jackets

The best baking potatoes are large and floury, such as King Edward, Maris Piper, Romano or Kerr's Pink.

BASIC BAKED POTATO
SERVES 4

Preheat oven to 200°C / 400°F / gas 6. Prick skins of 4 large scrubbed and dried floury potatoes and bake 1–1½ hours. Wearing an oven mitt, squeeze gently – they should feel soft. Cut a cross in top, and fluff flesh with fork. Add 50 g / 2 oz butter and season.

VARIATION: Microwaving is faster but finishing in oven gives skin right texture. Prepare the potatoes as above, then rub with olive oil and salt. Cook according to microwave cooker instructions. Transfer to oven and bake for 15–20 minutes.

BLUE CHEESE AND HERB JACKETS
SERVES 4

Bake 4 potatoes as above and cool slightly (leave oven on). Heat 25 g / 1 oz butter in a pan and cook 1 crushed garlic clove and 2 chopped spring onions for 2 minutes. Remove potato flesh, leaving skin intact, and mash. Fold in garlic mixture with 4 tablespoons sour cream, 115 g / 4 oz diced dolcelatte, 1 tablespoon each chopped parsley and chives. Season and spoon into skins, piling it high. Bake 10–15 minutes.

SPINACH, MUSHROOM AND EGG JACKETS
SERVES 2

Heat 1 tablespoon olive oil in a pan and fry 1 small finely chopped onion and 2 crushed garlic cloves for 3–5 minutes. Add 175 g / 6 oz sliced mushrooms and cook until golden. Season. Add 225 g / 8 oz spinach and simmer 3–4 minutes until liquid evaporates. Add 3 tablespoons mascarpone and cook 2 minutes. Cut a cross in top of each of 2 baked potatoes and squeeze open. Fluff flesh with a fork. Spoon in mixture, making a hollow. Crack an egg into each, season, and cover with foil. Bake 10–15 minutes until whites are set. Sprinkle with grated Parmesan.

AUBERGINE CHILLI JACKETS
SERVES 4

Heat 2 tablespoons oil and fry 1 sliced red onion 4–5 minutes. Dice 200 g / 8 oz aubergine and 1 red pepper, add and cook 5–8 minutes. Stir in 1 small finely chopped red chilli, 2 finely chopped garlic cloves and 1 teaspoon ground cumin. Add a large can of chopped tomatoes, 1 teaspoon tomato purée, a drained large can of kidney beans and 300 ml / ½ pint water. Simmer 15–20 minutes until vegetables are soft. Season. Fluff the flesh of 4 hot baked potatoes. Spoon over the chilli and top with 100 g / 4 oz grated smoked Cheddar.

HUMMUS AND AVOCADO SALSA JACKETS
SERVES 4

Dice ¼ cucumber, 2 plum tomatoes, 1 red onion and a peeled avocado and mix well. Whisk together juice of 1 lemon, 2 tablespoons extra-virgin olive oil and 3 tablespoons chopped coriander. Season and pour over salsa. Split 4 potatoes baked as above and fluff flesh. Spoon in 225 g / 8 oz hummus and top with salsa.

Oven Egg and Chips

PREPARATION: 10 MINUTES

COOKING: 40-45 MINUTES

SERVES 2

450 g/1 lb floury potatoes, such as King Edward or Maris Piper, scrubbed

2 garlic cloves, peeled and sliced

4 rosemary sprigs or 1 tsp dried

2 tbsp olive oil

salt and pepper

2 eggs

1 Preheat the oven to 220°C/425°F/gas 7. Cut the potatoes into thick chips.

2 Tip the chips into a roasting tin (a non-stick tin is best). Sprinkle over the sliced garlic. Strip the rosemary leaves from the sprigs and sprinkle the leaves over. Drizzle with the olive oil and season. Toss to coat the chips in the oil and all the flavourings.

3 Bake the chips for 35–40 minutes, until they are just cooked and golden in colour, shaking the pan about halfway through.

4 Make two gaps in the chips and break an egg into each gap. Return to the oven for 3–5 minutes, until the eggs are cooked to your liking.

VARIATIONS: If you can get a hold of some, a little goose fat used instead of the oil will give you the most delicious results. Instead of the rosemary, you can flavour the chips with some dried thyme, or a little chilli or curry powder.

Spiced Roast Potatoes

Sweet potatoes are delicious roasted but they cook more quickly than normal potatoes, so you will need to par-boil the floury potatoes for a few minutes, to soften them, before roasting them with the sweet ones.

PREPARATION: 15 MINUTES

COOKING: 1 HOUR

SERVES 4

450 g/1 lb floury potatoes, unpeeled

450 g/1 lb sweet potatoes, peeled

4 tbsp olive oil

25 g/1 oz butter

1 tsp ground turmeric

1 tsp chilli powder

1 tsp garam masala

1 tsp light muscovado sugar

salt and pepper

2 tbsp chopped fresh coriander

1 Preheat the oven to 200°C/400°F/gas 6. Place the floury potatoes in a pan, cover with cold water and bring to the boil. Simmer for 10 minutes, then drain and pat dry. Leave to cool slightly, then peel away the skins. Cut the floury potatoes and sweet potatoes into equal-sized cubes.

2 Place the oil and butter in a roasting tin and heat until the butter has melted and is foaming. Add the spices and sugar. Mix well. Add the potatoes to the tin, coating them all over in the oil and spices.

3 Roast for 40–50 minutes until tender. Season well and sprinkle with the coriander.

Steps to making Garlic and Rosemary Roasties (opposite), with and without the red onions.

Roast Potatoes

Most potatoes are good for roasting but Cara, Desirée, King Edward and Maris Piper are particularly good. They hold their shape when cooked, giving a delicious floury centre with crispy edges.

To ensure crispy potatoes, make sure they are completely dry before going into the oven. Resist the urge to turn the potatoes too often. Allow them to brown on one side before turning. Do not salt the potatoes until the end of cooking – salting beforehand encourages them to give up their liquid, making them limp.

PREPARATION: 10 MINUTES
COOKING: 1 HOUR
SERVES 4
900 g / 2 lb floury potatoes, unpeeled
3 tbsp olive oil
salt and pepper

1 Preheat oven to 200°C / 400°F / gas 6. Place potatoes in a pan, cover with cold salted water, bring to boil and cook for 10–15 minutes until tender, gently shaking the pan halfway through. Drain well and let cool slightly, then peel away skin. Cut potatoes into even-sized pieces.
2 Heat the oil in a roasting tin until very hot, then add the potatoes. Turn them so that they are evenly coated with oil.
3 Roast for 30 minutes. Remove from oven, turn and roast for 15–20 minutes more, or until brown and crunchy on the outside. Season well.

Red Onion, Garlic and Rosemary Roasties

These mouthwatering potatoes are a fine accompaniment to anything from a roast to a cheese soufflé. The key is to use small, firm potatoes – the smaller they are cut, the quicker they will cook.

PREPARATION: 10 MINUTES

COOKING: 30–35 MINUTES

SERVES 4

750 g / 1 lb 10 oz small, firm roasting potatoes

25 g / 1 oz butter

2 tbsp olive oil

2 red onions, cut into chunks

8 garlic cloves, unpeeled

2 tbsp chopped fresh rosemary

salt and pepper

1 Preheat the oven to 230°C / 450°F / gas 8. Peel the potatoes and quarter them. Rinse well and pat dry thoroughly.

2 Place the butter and oil in a roasting tin and heat in the oven until the butter has melted and is foaming. Add the potatoes, red onions, garlic and rosemary and toss well, making sure the potatoes and onions are sitting in a single layer.

3 Place the tin in the oven and roast for about 25 minutes, shaking the tin occasionally to turn the potatoes, until golden and tender when tested with a fork.

4 When the potatoes are cooked, season to taste with sea salt and freshly ground black pepper.

Hasselback Potatoes

Hasselback Potatoes are called after the Stockholm restaurant of the same name. Versions of this dish are also known by various descriptive terms, like 'hedgehog potatoes' or even 'toast-rack' potatoes.

PREPARATION: 10 MINUTES
COOKING: 1 HOUR 10 MINUTES
SERVES 4
900 g / 2 lb potatoes
1 tbsp sunflower oil
50 g / 2 oz butter
1 tsp paprika
coarse sea salt

1 Preheat the oven to 200°C / 400°F / gas 6. Peel the potatoes and place them in a pan of cold salted water. Bring to the boil and simmer for 10–15 minutes, then drain well and pat dry.
2 Beginning 1 cm / ½ inch in from the end, carefully make cuts 3 mm / ⅛ inch apart along the potato, but without cutting all the way through.
3 Heat the oil and butter in a small pan and add the paprika.
4 Place the potatoes in a roasting tin and brush them with the flavoured oil and butter. Roast for 40–50 minutes until golden brown and tender.
5 Serve sprinkled with the sea salt.

VARIATIONS: You can roast the hasselback potatoes on a bed of peeled garlic cloves for even more flavour. Try replacing the paprika with chilli powder or some dried rosemary. You could also consider stuffing the cuts in the potatoes with some tapenade, chopped anchovies, or slices of a melting cheese, such as Brie or mozzarella.

Scalloped Potato and Rich Cheese Flan

This dish is made with Tourée de l'Aubier, a cheese ripened in a spruce bark ring, giving it a tangy flavour. You could use Vacherin, Camembert or Reblochon instead.

PREPARATION: 15 MINUTES
COOKING: 55 MINUTES.
SERVES 4 AS A SUPPER DISH, OR 6 AS A SIDE DISH
425 ml / ¾ pint milk
142 ml / ¼ pint carton of double cream
1 garlic clove
1.3 kg / 3 lb potatoes, sliced into thin rounds
pinch of freshly grated nutmeg
200 g / 8 oz Tourée de l'Aubier (see above)
25 g / 1 oz butter, softened
salt and pepper

1 In a large, deep heavy casserole or frying pan, bring the milk and cream to a gentle simmer with the garlic, then add the potatoes in two batches to poach gently, uncovered, for 5 minutes until almost cooked but not falling apart. Lift out the slices with a slotted spoon and transfer to a plate. Remove the garlic when soft (with the first batch) and reserve.
2 Preheat the oven to 200°C / 400°F / gas 6. Drain any excess milk from the potatoes back into the pan and add nutmeg.
3 Wipe the cheese with kitchen paper, pare away any hard bits of rind and cut the cheese into slices. Add one-third of the slices to the milk and heat until melted. There will be bits of the rind, but it is fine to leave them in.
4 Crush the softened garlic clove and mash into the butter. Use to grease a 24 × 30 cm / 9½ × 12 inch ovenproof gratin dish. Lay a third of the potato slices overlapping in the bottom of the dish. Lay half remaining cheese slices on top. Pour over one-third of the cheesy milk mixture, season and continue layering in the same way. Don't fill the dish more than two-thirds full, as it will bubble up. Pour the remaining milk mixture over the final potato layer. Season lightly.
5 Bake for about 50 minutes, until golden brown in colour and cooked through.

There are hundreds of different potato varieties, and each country has developed varieties to suit tastes and growing conditions. Shops now sell far more types, making it possible to experiment.

For the cook, all varieties fall into one of two basic types – waxy and floury. Waxy potatoes are suitable for boiling and serving whole in salads; varieties grown in Britain include new and early potatoes, such as Pentland Javelin, Nadine, Arran Comet, Ulster Prince and Concorde. Marfona and the red-skinned Desirée are also waxy. Floury varieties are best for baking, mashing, roasting and deep-frying. They include Maris Piper, King Edward, Fianna, Golden Wonder, Cara and Morene.

New potatoes, with their thin flaky skins, should be used within a few days of purchase. Varieties include Maris Bard, Duke of York, and the famous Jersey Royals.

Speciality salad potatoes came only recently into the shops and include Charlotte, La Ratte, Pink Fir Apple and Anya. Then there are blue, black and purple curiosities such as Shetland Blacks, Edzell Blues and Purple Congos. Some are imported from France, and all are best simply boiled and tossed in butter and herbs. Cooking blue potatoes in the microwave helps to preserve their colour.

Potatoes

Potatoes Sautéed with Garlic and Onion

PREPARATION: 15 MINUTES
COOKING: 35 MINUTES
SERVES 4

1 Cook 900 g / 2 lb waxy new potatoes, unpeeled, in boiling salted water for about 10 minutes until almost soft. Drain, peel and cut into even-sized dice if very large.

2 Heat 2 tablespoons of olive oil and 50 g / 2 oz butter in a heavy-based frying pan and add the potatoes. Fry for 10 minutes until beginning to brown.

3 Add 1 onion, thinly sliced, and 3 garlic cloves, finely chopped. Cook for a further 5 minutes until crisp and golden.

4 Serve sprinkled with 2 tablespoons of chopped parsley, and some salt and pepper.

Pan Haggerty

Slice the potatoes for this layered cake on a mandolin grater or use the slicing attachment on a food processor. This way the slices will be of an even thickness so they will all cook in the same time.

PREPARATION: 15 MINUTES
COOKING: 50 MINUTES
SERVES 4

450 g / 1 lb firm potatoes
3 tbsp sunflower oil
1 medium onion, thinly sliced
115 g / 4 oz Cheddar cheese, grated
salt and pepper

1 Peel the potatoes and cut them into very thin slices (see above). Rinse the slices well and pat them dry on kitchen paper.
2 Heat the oil gently in a non-stick frying pan and make layers of potatoes, onion and cheese, seasoning between each layer and finishing with a layer of potatoes. Cook over a gentle heat for 30 minutes until the bottom is browned, then turn over (as for the Rösti, see overleaf) and brown for a further 20 minutes.
3 Serve cut into wedges.

VARIATIONS: Add a layer of sliced tomato between the onion and the cheese for a more moist dish. Replace half the potatoes with slices of celeriac for a delicious accompaniment to game dishes. You can use most melting hard cheeses instead of the Cheddar – Red Leicester, Gruyère and Caerphilly produce particularly nice results.

Stoved New Potatoes and Mushrooms

This way of cooking new potatoes is adapted from an old Scottish recipe, traditionally using meat stock. Here, the savouriness comes instead from dried mushrooms and their soaking liquid and olives. The potatoes are eaten smeared with the garlic, which cooks to a deliciously mild finish.

PREPARATION: 10 MINUTES
COOKING: 25 MINUTES
SERVES 2

1 tbsp crumbled dried porcini mushrooms
300 ml / $^1/_2$ pint hot vegetable stock
1 tbsp olive oil
4 plump garlic cloves, unpeeled
8 black olives
2 small sprigs of fresh rosemary, plus more to serve
500 g / 1 lb 2 oz new potatoes, cut into 5 mm / $^1/_4$ inch slices
100 g / 4 oz chestnut mushrooms, sliced
salt and pepper
chopped fresh flat-leaf parsley, to serve (optional)

1 Place the crumbled mushrooms in a jug and pour over the hot stock. Leave to soak while you prepare the vegetables.
2 Heat the oil in a heavy frying pan with a lid. Add the whole garlic cloves, olives and rosemary and cook for 2 minutes.
3 Add half the potatoes, to cover the base of the pan. Remove the porcini mushrooms from the liquid with a slotted spoon and scatter, with the chestnut mushrooms, over the potatoes. Cover with the remaining potatoes. Pour the reserved mushroom liquid over and add plenty of seasoning.
4 Cover and cook for 15 minutes more. Remove the lid and cook for a further 5 minutes, until the potatoes are tender and almost all the liquid has been absorbed.
5 Divide between 2 warmed serving plates. Discard the rosemary, adding fresh leaves with the flat-leaf parsley, if liked.
6 To eat, cut off the end of each of the garlic cloves and press out the creamy flesh to eat with the potatoes.

Potato Rösti

Traditionally made as one large flat cake, you can also make individual rösti.

PREPARATION: 10 MINUTES
COOKING: 30 MINUTES
SERVES 4
900 g / 2 lb potatoes, unpeeled
salt and pepper
25 g / 1 oz butter
1 tbsp olive oil

1 Cook the potatoes in boiling salted water for 10 minutes until almost soft. Remove from the pan, and allow to cool in their skins. Peel away the skins and grate the flesh coarsely. Season.

2 In a 23 cm / 9 inch non-stick frying pan, heat the butter and oil until very hot. Spread the potato evenly in the pan, reduce the heat and cook gently for 10 minutes.

3 Turn the rösti over by placing a plate or board over the pan and inverting it on to the plate. Slide it back into the pan, cooked-side up, and continue to cook for a further 10 minutes until cooked underneath.

4 Serve cut into wedges.

Potato Latkes with Herb-grilled Feta

Latke *is the Jewish name for a pancake made with grated potatoes, similar to* rösti. *This particular treatment is by Paul Gayler.*

PREPARATION: 25 MINUTES
COOKING: 55 MINUTES
SERVES 4
1 large potato, peeled and coarsely grated
1 onion, coarsely grated
1 medium egg, beaten
25 g / 1 oz plain flour
2 tbsp vegetable oil
2 tsp small capers, drained, to serve
FOR THE CHILLI JAM:
25 g / 1 oz butter
2 onions, thinly sliced
50 g / 2 oz caster sugar
6 tbsp red wine vinegar
1 red chilli, deseeded and finely chopped
FOR THE HERB-GRILLED FETA:
6 tbsp olive oil
1 garlic clove, crushed
1 tsp each chopped fresh oregano and thyme
salt and pepper
250 g / 9 oz feta cheese

1 To make the chilli jam: heat the butter in a pan, add the onions and cook for 6–8 minutes until golden and softened. Add the sugar and red wine vinegar and cook gently for a further 25 minutes. Add the chilli and cook for a further 5–10 minutes until the onions are caramelized and bright red in colour. Keep the mixture hot.

2 Meanwhile, make the latkes. Take the grated potato in your hands and squeeze together to extract as much moisture and starch as possible. Pat dry on kitchen paper, then place in a bowl. Add the onion, beaten egg and flour and mix well.

3 Heat half the oil in a large non-stick frying pan, divide the potato mixture into 4 and add 2 of these portions to the pan. Flatten slightly and fry for 3–4 minutes on each side until crisp and golden. Keep warm. Heat the remaining oil and cook the other two portions. Keep warm.

4 To make the herb-grilled feta: preheat the grill and mix together the olive oil, garlic, oregano, thyme and seasoning. Cut the feta into 4 equal slices, arrange these in a grill pan and coat with half the olive oil mixture. Grill for 2–3 minutes until slightly melted.

5 To serve, place the latkes on serving plates and top with a spoonful of the chilli jam. Place the grilled feta on top, sprinkle over a few capers and drizzle over a little of the remaining olive oil mixture.

Soufflé Potatoes

These are thin rounds of potato cooked in exactly the same way as chips until they are puffed up and golden.

When choosing oil for deep-frying, you need to use one that has a relatively high smoke-point, i.e., it can be heated to a high temperature before starting to break down. It should also be relatively flavourless, so that its flavour will not overpower that of the potato or other food being fried. Sunflower, groundnut or a pure vegetable oil are ideal.

PREPARATION: 15 MINUTES
COOKING: 10–15 MINUTES
SERVES 4

3 medium floury potatoes
groundnut oil for deep-frying
salt

1 Peel the potatoes and cut them into 5-mm / ¼-inch slices (slightly thicker than that required for potato crisps). Wipe them dry – do not put them in water!
2 Heat the oil to 190°C / 375°F and fry the potato slices in batches for 1–2 minutes. Drain on kitchen paper and repeat with the remaining potatoes.
3 Heat the oil until very hot (200°C / 400°F), then add the potatoes to the oil, again in batches. They will puff up and brown. Drain each batch well.
4 Serve the soufflé potatoes sprinkled with salt.

VARIATION: For an attractive multicoloured special occasion accompaniment, try making these with a mixture of sliced roots, including celeriac, parsnips and beetroot.

Chips

The size of the chip determines how much fat is absorbed. Thin-cut chips have a greater surface area compared to their centres, and are therefore a lot quite a lot higher in fat than fat wedges of chips.

PREPARATION: 15 MINUTES
COOKING: 10–15 MINUTES
SERVES 4

groundnut oil for deep-frying
4 large potatoes
salt

1 Preheat the oven to 160°C / 325°F / gas 3. Half fill a heavy-based, medium-sized pan or chip pan with the oil, or begin to heat the oil in a deep-fat fryer.

2 Peel the potatoes, rinse and cut into strips about 1 cm / ¹/₂ inch wide and 5 cm / 2 inches long, setting them aside in a bowl of cold water once prepared.

3 Thoroughly dry a batch of cut potatoes on kitchen paper. To test that the oil is ready, drop in a cube of bread; if it sizzles and turns brown in 5–10 seconds, the oil is hot enough. Alternatively, if you have a cooking thermometer, the temperature of the oil at this stage should be 190°C / 375°F. Place the chips in a chip basket and lower into the oil. Fry for 5–6 minutes, shaking the basket a few times to ensure even cooking. Lift out and drain on kitchen paper. Continue to cook the remaining potatoes.

4 Heat the oil to very hot (200°C / 400°F) and fry the part-cooked chips, in batches, in the hot oil for 2–3 minutes until browned. Drain thoroughly on kitchen paper and place on a hot serving plate. Keep hot in the oven (with its door open so they don't go soggy) while you cook the remaining chips in the same way.

5 When all the chips are ready, serve sprinkled with salt.

Mash and More

Choose from Golden Wonder, King Edward, Maris Piper and Wilja potatoes when planning to mash. For the best mash, cook the potatoes whole and unpeeled to prevent them from becoming waterlogged.

BASIC MASHED POTATO

SERVES 4

Cook 900 g / 2 lb unpeeled potatoes in boiling salted water. Drain and, when cool enough, peel and return to the pan with 50 g / 2 oz butter. Mash over gentle heat until smooth. Gradually add 150 ml / $^{1}/_{4}$ pint hot milk and beat until smooth and creamy. Season.

ALIGOT

SERVES 4

Make the mash as above, adding 4 tablespoons double cream with the butter. Mash over a gentle heat. Instead of milk, beat in a crushed garlic clove, then add 175 g / 6 oz grated Gruyère, a little at a time. The potatoes are ready when they are shiny and come away from sides of the pan. Season well.

LEEK AND MUSTARD MASH

SERVES 4

Heat 2 tablespoons olive oil in a pan and fry 2 large leeks, finely chopped, for 7–10 minutes. Fork into Basic Mashed Potato as above with 2 tablespoons wholegrain mustard and 100 g / 4 oz grated Cheddar.

HERB AND PARMESAN MASH

SERVES 4

Mix 50 g / 2 oz grated Parmesan into the Basic Mashed Potato as above. Beat in a further large knob of butter together with 3 tablespoons each chopped parsley and basil. Season to taste.

CHAMP

SERVES 4

For this classic Irish dish, first chop a bunch of spring onions, including the green tops, and put in a pan with 300 ml / $^{1}/_{2}$ pint milk. Bring to the boil, reduce the heat and simmer for 2–3 minutes. Remove from the heat and leave to infuse for about 10 minutes.

Use to make the Basic Mashed Potato as above, instead of the plain hot milk. Reheat, if necessary, in a clean pan and then spoon into small serving bowls.

Make a hollow in the top of each and add some more butter and some crumbled blue cheese if you like. Dip forkfuls of the mashed potato in the melted butter (and cheese) to eat.

COLCANNON

SERVES 4

To make this other traditional Irish treat, replace the spring onions in the Champ with some shredded cabbage or kale. You can serve it like the Champ, but without the blue cheese, with melted butter, or fry it in the butter in small flat cakes.

CLAPSHOT

SERVES 4

This Scottish dish is made like Champ but without cheese and using equal quantities of potato and swedes ('neeps' in Scotland). Beat in some chopped chives or bacon fat for extra flavour, if you like. The spring onions are optional.

Perhaps no one makes better use of vegetable crunch, colour and vigour than the cuisines of the Orient. There it is traditional generally to cook vegetables only briefly to preserve their many properties. Enjoy steaming stir-fries; flavour-packed noodle dishes and piquant salads, as well as subtly spiced curries and crisp mouthwatering fillings for spring rolls.

Stirring it up

Oriental Ways with Vegetables

Spring Vegetable Noodles

PREPARATION: 15 MINUTES

COOKING: 10–15 MINUTES

SERVES 4

2 tbsp olive oil

1 tbsp chopped fresh parsley

1 egg, beaten

250 g / 9 oz medium egg noodles

2 garlic cloves, finely chopped

5 cm / 2 inch piece of root ginger, cut into sticks

2 carrots, cut into sticks

115 g / 4 oz chestnut mushrooms, thickly sliced

115 g / 4 oz sugar snap peas

200 g / 8 oz leeks, sliced into strips

2 tbsp soy sauce

150 ml / 1/4 pint vegetable stock

1 Heat half the oil in a large frying pan. Mix the parsley and egg and pour into the pan to make a thin omelette. Cook for 1 minute until set, flip and cook for 30 seconds more. Put on a plate.

2 Cook the noodles according to the packet instructions.

3 Meanwhile, heat the remaining oil in the pan, toss in the garlic and ginger and stir-fry over a moderate heat for 30 seconds. Add the carrots and mushrooms and fry over a high heat for a few minutes, stirring occasionally. Add the sugar snap peas and the leeks and stir-fry for 2 minutes. Season. Pour in the soy sauce and stock and cook over a high heat for about 1 minute.

4 Cut the omelette into thin strips. When the noodles are ready, drain and fork on to serving plates. Top with the vegetables in their juices and pile the omelette strips on top.

Udon Noodles with Miso and Roast Ginger Pumpkin

You can use frozen or dried udon noodles, both available from Chinese supermarkets, for Mark Gregory's recipe. You will also find vacuum-packed noodles in major supermarkets.

PREPARATION: 25 MINUTES

COOKING: 45 MINUTES

SERVES 4

600 ml / 1 pint vegetable stock

1 tbsp dark miso paste

4 tbsp soy sauce

250 g / 9 oz Japanese udon noodles

1 head of bok choi or pak choi, leaves separated

1 leek, trimmed, halved and shredded

3 cm / 1 1/4 inch piece of fresh root ginger, peeled and finely shredded

4 spring onions, trimmed and sliced

1 tbsp fresh coriander leaves, to garnish

2 tsp toasted sesame oil (optional)

FOR THE ROAST GINGER PUMPKIN:

800 g / 1 lb 12 oz pumpkin, peeled, deseeded and cut into bite-sized pieces

3 tbsp vegetable oil

2 tbsp grated fresh root ginger

sea salt flakes

1 First prepare the pumpkin: preheat the oven to 200°C / 400°F / gas 6. Place the pumpkin in a large roasting tin and toss with the oil, ginger and sea salt. Roast for 40 minutes, until golden and softened.

2 Mix together the stock, miso paste and soy sauce in a pan. Stir in the noodles, bok choi or pak choi, leek, pumpkin, ginger and spring onions and cook for 3 minutes until the noodles are heated through.

3 Divide between 4 warm serving bowls and ladle the broth over. Scatter the coriander on top and drizzle over sesame oil, if liked, before serving.

Hoisin Chinese Noodles

A pack of noodles and a few dried shiitake mushrooms help make a tasty meal from oddments of fresh or canned vegetables. Most Oriental-style noodles are suitable for this dish, but check the instructions, as some might need pre-cooking rather than just soaking.

PREPARATION: 20 MINUTES
COOKING: 10 MINUTES
SERVES 4

50 g / 2 oz dried shiitake mushrooms
250 g / 9 oz medium egg noodles
3 tbsp sesame oil
2 garlic cloves, crushed
$^1/_2$ tsp finely chopped fresh root ginger
bunch of spring onions, roughly chopped
140 g / 5 oz sugar snap peas
100 g / 4 oz asparagus tips
200 g / 8 oz tofu, diced
150 ml / $^1/_4$ pint hoisin sauce (Chinese barbecue sauce)
2 tbsp soy sauce
salt and pepper
fresh coriander leaves, to garnish

1 Rinse the mushrooms, then soak them in tepid water for 30 minutes. Drain, reserving the liquid, and roughly chop. Soak the noodles according to the packet instructions. Drain thoroughly.
2 Heat the oil in a large non-stick frying pan or wok over a high heat. Add the garlic, ginger and mushrooms and, as soon as they sizzle, toss in the remaining vegetables and stir-fry for 3 minutes.
3 Add the diced tofu, 2 tablespoons of the reserved mushroom soaking liquid, the hoisin sauce and soy sauce. Stir-fry until the sauce boils, then tip in the drained noodles. Toss together over the heat until piping hot. Season to taste.
4 Serve garnished with fresh coriander leaves.

VARIATIONS: Replace the tofu with 85 g / 3 oz roasted cashew nuts, or add protein in the form of a three-egg omelette, rolled and sliced, scattered over the finished stir-fry.

You can choose French beans, baby corn cobs, sliced peppers or bean sprouts instead of sugar snap peas and asparagus.

Vegetable Stir-fry with Filo 'Noodles'

The texture of tofu is improved by brisk stir-frying. Crunchy filo pastry 'noodles' make a healthy alternative to fried noodles.

PREPARATION: 15 MINUTES

COOKING: ABOUT 15 MINUTES

SERVES 2

150 g / 5^1/$_2$ oz marinated tofu cubes

4 sheets of filo pastry

1 tbsp oil

^{1}/$_2$ tsp cornflour

6 fat spring onions, thickly sliced

1 red pepper, deseeded and sliced

140 g / 5 oz broccoli, cut into small florets

100 g / 4 oz fresh bean sprouts

FOR THE MARINADE:

1 garlic clove, crushed

2 cm / ^{3}/$_4$ inch piece of fresh root ginger, chopped

1 tbsp soy sauce

3 tbsp dry sherry or rice wine

2 tsp sweet chilli sauce

1 Preheat the oven to 190°C / 375°F / gas 5. Make the marinade: mix the ingredients together in a shallow glass dish. Toss the tofu in the soy mixture to coat and leave to marinate while you prepare the remaining ingredients.

2 Roll up the filo sheets and slice into 1 cm / ^{1}/$_2$ inch wide ribbons. Use your fingers to separate them and spread them out evenly on a baking sheet. Cook for 8 minutes until crisp and pale golden.

3 Meanwhile, heat the oil in a wok or large pan. Lift the tofu out of the marinade with a slotted spoon and stir-fry for 2 minutes. Reserve the marinade.

4 Mix the cornflour with 2 tablespoons water and stir into the marinade. Remove the tofu from the wok and return to the marinade.

5 Add the spring onions, pepper and broccoli to the wok and stir-fry for 2 minutes. Add the bean sprouts and tip in the tofu mixture. Stir-fry until the marinade comes to the boil and thickens.

6 Divide the filo noodles between 2 plates and spoon the stir-fry on top. Serve immediately.

Lime-yellow, flame-orange, pillar-box red and nightshade purple – and every shade in between, there are 3,000-odd varieties of chilli, and they open up a whole new world of flavour. Chillies originated in South America, but their unique properties quickly won them a pivotal role in the cooking of most continents. Size, shape and colour are little guide to either heat or flavour; although, in general, the smaller they are the hotter they tend to be. The Habanero or Scotch bonnet is probably the hottest known, thin red and green Thai peppers have fairly good heat and an intriguing taste, while the torpedo-shaped Jalapeño is medium-hot and has bags of good fruity flavour.

Look for firm glossy specimens, with no trace of mould or looseness about the stems. Store them in loose plastic bags in the salad drawer of the fridge. The heat of the chilli lies in the capsaicin, the oily substance found in the seeds and the pale membrane that connects them to the flesh; so some or all of these should be removed before use if you don't want too fierce a result. Wash your hands carefully after you have handled chillies as the capsaicin can burn sensitive areas like the eyes.

Chillies

Chilli Oil

Use this easy-to-make chilli oil as a flavouring – add a drop to salad dressings or cooked pasta, brush it over grilled fish or stir a little into tomato-based sauces. You could also float a fresh chilli in the oil and serve it as a condiment.

1 Gently heat 600 ml / 1 pint vegetable or corn oil in a saucepan.
2 Halve 4 fresh, medium-hot red chillies, lengthwise and cook gently for 5 minutes. You can leave the seeds in or remove some or all of them, depending on how hot you want the chilli oil to be. Set aside overnight for the flavour and colour to develop.
3 Next day, strain the oil into sterilized bottles and seal. Store for up to 6 months.

Brussels Sprout Satay

PREPARATION: 10 MINUTES

COOKING: ABOUT 10 MINUTES

SERVES 4

500 g / 1 lb 2 oz Brussels sprouts

1 tbsp smooth peanut butter

5 tbsp Japanese soy sauce

2 tbsp sunflower oil

4 tbsp toasted pine nuts, roughly chopped

1 In a pan of boiling water, cook the Brussels sprouts for about 5–6 minutes until just tender; drain well.

2 In a small bowl, mix the peanut butter with 4 tablespoons of the soy sauce and stir until you have a smooth paste.

3 Heat the oil in a wok or large frying pan, then quickly stir-fry the sprouts for 2 minutes. Remove from the heat and stir half the peanut soy paste into the pan.

4 Transfer to a serving dish. Drizzle with the remaining paste and the tablespoon of soy sauce and sprinkle with the pine nuts. Serve either warm or cold.

Thai Spring Rolls with Chilli Dipping Sauce

You can buy spring roll wrappers chilled or frozen in Chinese food stores and some supermarkets.

PREPARATION: 20 MINUTES

COOKING: 10 MINUTES

MAKES 12

2 small courgettes

2 tbsp groundnut oil

2 spring onions, thinly sliced

4 shiitake mushrooms, stems removed,
　　caps thinly sliced

100 g / 4 oz bean sprouts

4–6 sprigs each of fresh basil, mint and
　　watercress, leaves cut into thin slivers

1 tsp dark soy sauce

2 tbsp mirin (Japanese rice wine), or 1 tbsp
　　each dry sherry and water, mixed together

1 cm / $\frac{1}{2}$ inch piece of fresh root ginger,
　　finely chopped

salt and pepper

12 spring roll wrappers

1 egg, beaten

oil, for deep-frying

FOR THE CHILLI DIPPING SAUCE:

1 tbsp each soy sauce, groundnut oil
　　and lime juice

1 small hot chilli, deseeded and thinly sliced

1 Cut each courgette across into 8 thick slices, then cut each slice into thin sticks.

2 Heat the groundnut oil in a frying pan, then cook the courgettes, onions, mushrooms, bean sprouts, basil, mint and watercress with the soy sauce, mirin and ginger until softened slightly (1–2 minutes). Season to taste.

3 Spoon a tablespoon of the mixture on one end of a spring roll wrapper and roll up, folding in the ends and brushing with beaten egg to help it stick. Repeat to make 12.

4 Fill a wok one-third full with oil and heat until a stale bread cube dropped into the oil turns golden brown after about 15 seconds. (Or heat the oil in a deep-fat fryer to 180°C / 350°F.) Deep-fry the rolls, 4 at a time, for about 1–2 minutes until golden brown, turning from time to time. Remove with a slotted spoon and drain on kitchen paper.

5 Mix together the dipping sauce ingredients in a bowl.

6 Serve the spring rolls with the dipping sauce.

Green Vegetable Curry with Shiitake Mushrooms

Jars of Thai green curry paste and fresh shiitake mushrooms are now available from better supermarkets.

PREPARATION: 7 MINUTES

COOKING: 10 MINUTES

SERVES 4

300 ml / $^1/_2$ pint coconut milk, plus 2 tbsp more
   for garnish

40 g / 1 $^1/_2$ oz Thai green curry paste

300 ml / $^1/_2$ pint vegetable stock

8 baby aubergines, halved lengthwise

225 g / 8 oz yard-long or French beans, cut into
   2.5 cm / 1 inch lengths

1 tsp palm sugar or light muscovado sugar

1 tsp fish sauce or soy sauce

5 mm / $^1/_4$ inch piece of fresh root ginger,
   peeled and chopped

115 g / 4 oz shiitake mushrooms, sliced

fresh basil and coriander leaves, to garnish

1 Heat the 300 ml / $^1/_2$ pint coconut milk in a saucepan with the curry paste. Stir to amalgamate.

2 Add the stock and then the aubergines, beans, sugar, fish or soy sauce, ginger and mushrooms. Bring to the boil and simmer, stirring, for 3-4 minutes. Adjust the seasoning with more sugar and fish or soy sauce as necessary.

3 Serve in bowls, garnished with the basil and coriander leaves and drizzled with the extra coconut milk.

Spicy Green Lentils with Crispy Onions

PREPARATION: 20 MINUTES

COOKING: 45 MINUTES

SERVES 2 AS A MAIN COURSE

WITH PARATHAS (OVERLEAF)

175 g / 6 oz whole green lentils

$^1/_4$ tsp each ground turmeric, chilli powder and
   fenugreek seeds

5 mm / $^1/_4$ inch piece of fresh root ginger, grated

$^3/_4$ tsp salt

1 medium tomato, chopped

1 tbsp ghee or vegetable oil

1 tsp cumin seeds

3 whole cloves

3 garlic cloves, finely chopped

1 medium onion, sliced

$^1/_4$ tsp garam masala

1 tbsp fresh coriander leaves

1 Wash the lentils in a sieve. In a pan, combine the lentils, turmeric, chilli, fenugreek, ginger, 600 ml / 1 pint of water and the salt. Bring to the boil, cover and simmer for 40 minutes, by which time the water should all be absorbed (if necessary, a little extra water can be added during cooking). Stir in the tomato.

2 Meanwhile, heat the ghee or oil in a frying pan. Add the cumin seeds and cloves. When they crackle, add the garlic and onion. When the onion begins to brown and crisp, turn off the heat.

3 Bring the lentils to a gentle simmer and quickly add half the fried spice onion mixture and the oil. Sprinkle with the remaining onions, garam masala and coriander leaves.

Cabbage Paratha with Sesame Seeds

In India, normal everyday breads are not flavoured because they are eaten with spicy curries, but this north Indian unleavened bread has been gently flavoured with spices, so is more of a snack bread and goes well with a mild-flavoured lentil or vegetable dish.

PREPARATION: 30 MINUTES
COOKING: ABOUT 15 MINUTES
MAKES 8 PARATHAS
100 g / 4 oz wholewheat flour, plus extra for rolling and dusting
100 g / 4 oz plain flour
50 g / 2 oz white cabbage, very finely shredded
1 cm / 1/2 inch piece of fresh root ginger, peeled and grated
1/2 tsp chilli powder
1 tbsp sesame seeds
1/4 tsp turmeric
1/2 tsp dill seeds (optional)
1 tsp salt
1 tbsp vegetable oil, plus extra for brushing
125–150 ml / 4–5 fl oz warm water

1 In a bowl, combine the flours with the cabbage, ginger, chilli, sesame seeds, turmeric, dill seeds (if using) and salt. Stir in the tablespoon of vegetable oil, then gradually add 125 ml / 4 fl oz warm water, mixing everything to make a soft dough; add more water if necessary. Do not add all the water at once because if too much is added the dough will be very sticky and difficult to roll. Divide into 8 equal balls.
2 Heat a cast-iron frying pan or griddle until very hot. Flatten each ball and dust with flour. Roll each ball into a 15 cm / 6 inch disc on a pastry board or flat surface.
3 Slap the paratha on the hot griddle and cook for 45–60 seconds before turning it over. Brush the cooked side with oil, turn over again and cook for 20 seconds. Brush the second side with oil and turn again for 20 seconds.
4 Remove from the griddle and put on a plate. (Keep warm by covering loosely with a tea towel.) Repeat with the remaining dough balls. Serve hot or cold.

Cauliflower, Beans and Tomatoes with Mustard Seeds

PREPARATION: 15 MINUTES
COOKING: 20 MINUTES
SERVES 4 WITH OTHER DISHES
4 tbsp vegetable oil
1 tbsp black mustard seeds
1 small onion, finely chopped
3 garlic cloves, finely chopped
225g / 8oz cauliflower, cut into small florets
225g / 8oz green beans, cut into 4 cm / 1 1/2 inch lengths
1/2 tsp chilli powder
1/2 tsp ground turmeric
1 tsp each salt and sugar
1 cm / 1/2 inch piece of fresh root ginger, grated
12 cherry tomatoes, halved
1/2 tsp garam masala

1 Heat the oil in a frying pan, add the mustard seeds and fry until they pop. Add the onion and garlic and fry until golden. Stir in the cauliflower and beans and fry for 5 minutes until the florets begin to singe.
2 Add the chilli, turmeric, salt, sugar and ginger with 2 tablespoons of water. Cover and cook gently for 15 minutes. Add the tomatoes and cook for 2 minutes more.
3 Sprinkle with the garam masala and serve.

Opposite (clockwise from bottom left): Cauliflower, Beans and Tomatoes with Mustard Seeds; Spicy Green Lentils with Crispy Onions (page 143); Cabbage Paratha with Sesame Seeds

Festive Bites

Vegetables aren't normally the first type of ingredient that comes to mind when thinking of party food, but they are perfect candidates – making the best and most flavoursome of dips and providing the most unusual and colourful toppings for canapés. Even the canapé bases can be made from vegetables too, as in our mini roast potatoes with various tasty toppings.

Party Food

Garlic Sesame Dip with Crispy Pittas

You can buy jars of tahini paste from large supermarkets, as well as health food shops. The dip can be made the day before and stored in the fridge.

PREPARATION: ABOUT 20 MINUTES
COOKING: ABOUT 5 MINUTES
MAKES 50 SCOOPS
4 thick slices of white country bread, crusts removed, cut into cubes
1 tbsp tahini paste
2 garlic cloves, crushed
175 ml / 6 fl oz extra-virgin olive oil
2 tbsp fromage frais or Quark
juice of 1 lemon
salt and pepper
8 pitta breads, split in half
2 tsp toasted sesame seeds
selection of olives, to serve

1 Preheat the grill. Sprinkle the bread with water, then squeeze well and put in a food processor or blender with the tahini and garlic. Whizz until smooth, drizzling in the oil in a slow steady stream until the mixture forms a thick paste.
2 Transfer to a bowl and stir in the fromage frais or Quark, lemon juice and salt and pepper to taste.
3 Tear the pitta breads into rough pieces. Place on a baking sheet and grill for 4–5 minutes until lightly browned.
4 Sprinkle the dip with sesame seeds and serve with the crispy pittas and olives.

Pakoras with Spicy Yoghurt Dip

PREPARATION: 15 MINUTES
COOKING: 12–15 MINUTES
MAKES ABOUT 16
675 g / 1 1/2 lb mixed vegetables (e.g., potato, courgettes, peppers, okra, onion, aubergine), cut into 1 cm / 1/2 inch cubes
oil, for frying
FOR THE SPICY YOGHURT DIP:
1 small onion, quartered
1 garlic clove
15 g / 1/2 oz fresh coriander
1 red chilli, halved and deseeded
2 tbsp blanched almonds
1 tbsp lime juice
150 ml / 1/4 pint natural yoghurt
salt and pepper
FOR THE BATTER:
2 garlic cloves, crushed
1 tsp each ground cumin, coriander, turmeric, hot chilli powder and salt
2 tsp garam masala
150 g / 5 1/2 oz gram flour (chickpea flour)
2 tbsp sunflower oil
2 tbsp each chopped fresh mint and coriander

1 To make the dip, place the onion, garlic, coriander, chilli, almonds and lime juice in a food processor and process. Stir in the yoghurt and season to taste. Chill.
2 Mix all the batter ingredients with 225 ml / 8 fl oz cold water to make a smooth, thick batter. Season to taste.
3 Blanch any hard vegetables, such as carrots or potatoes, in lightly salted boiling water for 2–3 minutes. Drain well. Stir into the batter with the rest of the vegetables and coat well.
4 Heat 4 cm / 1 1/2 inches of oil in a pan until a cube of bread dropped into it rises to the surface and browns within 1 minute. Drop heaped tablespoons of the vegetable mixture into the hot oil and fry in batches for 2–3 minutes, turning occasionally, until golden. Drain on absorbent kitchen paper and keep hot.
5 Serve with the spicy yoghurt dip.

Hummus

PREPARATION: ABOUT 15 MINUTES

SERVES 4

two 420 g / 14 oz cans of chickpeas, drained

juice of 1 lemon

3 tbsp tahini paste (see opposite, optional)

2 tbsp olive oil, plus more to serve

2 garlic cloves, crushed

fresh flat-leaved parsley sprigs, to serve

1 Whizz the chickpeas in a blender or food processor until crumb-like.

2 Transfer to a bowl and beat in the lemon juice, tahini if using it, olive oil and garlic with a wooden spoon. If the mixture seems slightly heavy, add a little water to lighten it.

3 To serve, spoon into small dishes, pour a pool of olive oil in the centre and garnish with parsley.

Hummus Falafel

PREPARATION: 10 MINUTES

COOKING: 10 MINUTES

MAKES ABOUT 24

250 g / 9 oz ready-made hummus or see above

4 tbsp ground almonds

3 tbsp chopped fresh coriander, plus more leaves to garnish

2 tbsp lemon juice

salt and pepper

2 tbsp olive oil

1 In a bowl, mix together the hummus, almonds, coriander and 1 teaspoon of the lemon juice. Season to taste.

2 Take a tablespoon of the mixture and shape into a 3 cm / 1¼ inch round. Repeat with the remaining mixture.

3 Heat the oil in a frying pan and cook the falafel in batches for 2 minutes on each side until golden brown. Drain on kitchen paper.

4 Served topped with the extra whole coriander leaves, and with the remaining lemon juice sprinkled over.

TOP LEFT TO RIGHT Mushroom Frittata, Mini Crab Tortilla
MIDDLE LEFT TO RIGHT Pâté Crostini with Onion Marmalade, Smoked Salmon
and Horseradish Crostini, Mozzarella with Mediterranean Tomato Salsa
BOTTOM LEFT TO RIGHT Duck with Kumquat and Shallot Relish, Tomato Tartlets
with Pesto, Ham Rarebit with Gherkin Salad, Scallops and Sage Wrapped in Bacon

Canapé Cornucopia

MUSHROOM FRITTATA

MAKES 32

Preheat a hot grill. Beat together 6 eggs, 3 tablespoons double cream and 25 g / 1 oz finely grated Parmesan cheese. Season. Heat 2 tablespoons olive oil and 25 g / 1 oz butter in a small frying pan. Add 250 g / 9 oz sliced chestnut mushrooms and cook for 5 minutes until soft. Season. Spread mushrooms evenly over pan, pour over egg mixture and fry gently for 5 minutes. Sprinkle another 25 g / 1 oz grated Parmesan over the top and place pan under the grill for about 2 minutes until the frittata is puffed and golden on top. Serve hot or cold, cut into small wedges or cubes.

MINI CRAB TORTILLA

MAKES 20

Mix 175 g / 6 oz crab meat (fresh, defrosted frozen or drained canned) with 2 tablespoons sour cream, 1 tablespoon lime juice, 1 teaspoon Tabasco sauce and 1 finely chopped spring onion. Season. Deseed and finely chop 450 g / 1 lb tomatoes. Spoon a generous amount of crab mixture on each of 20 corn tortilla chips and top with spoonful of the chopped tomato.

PÂTÉ CROSTINI WITH ONION MARMALADE

MAKES 30

Preheat oven to 180°C / 350°F / gas 4. Cut a baguette into thirty 1 cm / ¹/₂ inch slices and bake for about 10 minutes until golden and crisp. Allow to cool. Meanwhile, heat 2 tablespoons olive oil in a frying pan and add 3 thinly sliced red onions, 2 teaspoons caster sugar,

3 tablespoons balsamic vinegar, ¹/₂ teaspoon ground star anise or five-spice powder and pinch of dried thyme. Cook gently, stirring occasionally, for 30 minutes until soft and caramelized. Let cool. To serve, place a small portion of coarse pâté (200 g / 7 oz in total) on each toast and top with the onion marmalade.

SMOKED SALMON AND HORSERADISH CROSTINI

MAKES 30

Preheat oven to 180°C / 350°F / gas 4. Slice a baguette and bake as for the Crostini above. Set aside to cool. Beat together 100 g / 4 oz each crème fraîche and creamed horseradish with 1 teaspoon each grated lemon zest and clear honey. Put a spoonful of mixture on each crostini, top with coil of smoked salmon (250 g / 9 oz in total) and garnish with dill sprigs to serve.

MOZZARELLA WITH MEDITERRANEAN TOMATO SALSA

MAKES 30

Heat 2 tablespoons olive oil in a small pan, add 1 teaspoon fennel seeds and heat gently for 1 minute. Remove from heat, stir in 1 teaspoon dried oregano and let cool. Stir 6 deseeded and chopped plum tomatoes, 10 halved stoned black olives and 1 tablespoon chopped parsley into the cooled oil and season. Cut 500 g / 1 lb 2 oz mozzarella cheese into thirty 5 mm / ¹/₄ inch slices and thinly slice ¹/₂ red onion. Top each slice of mozzarella with a spoonful of tomato salsa and 2 or 3 onion slices. Serve cold.

DUCK WITH KUMQUAT AND SHALLOT RELISH

MAKES 30

The day before: rub 2 trimmed duck legs with salt and 1 tablespoon five-spice powder. Place in a plastic bag. Mix 1 tablespoon each dark soy sauce and clear honey with 2 teaspoons dark sesame oil. Pour over duck in bag, seal and chill overnight. Next day, preheat oven to 180°C / 350°F / gas 4. In a small pan, gently heat 6 tablespoons olive oil with a bruised garlic clove for a few minutes. Leave to cool with garlic in. Slice a baguette, brush with the garlic-infused oil and bake as above. Let cool. Increase oven to 200°C / 400°F / gas 6 and roast duck for 50 minutes. Let cool, then shred meat from bones. Make relish by heating 2 tablespoons olive oil in a small pan and adding 8 small shallots, quartered, 1 small finely chopped red onion and 3 chopped garlic cloves. Cook for 5 minutes until golden. Add 1/2 tablespoon sugar and 2 tablespoons red wine vinegar and cook until reduced and caramelized. Add another tablespoon sugar and 10 kumquats, each cut into 8 wedges, with the juice of 2 oranges, 5 tablespoons water and season. Bring to a simmer and cook gently for 15 minutes until reduced to a relish consistency. Top each toast with a little relish and some shredded duck. Garnish with endive.

TOMATO TARTLETS WITH PESTO

MAKES 25

Preheat oven to 220°C / 425°F / gas 7. Roll out 250 g / 9 oz ready-made puff pastry to a thickness of 5 mm/1/4 inch. Stamp out 25 rounds slightly larger than the small tomatoes you are using and place on a baking sheet. Cut each of 5 tomatoes into 5 slices and place one on each pastry round. Brush tarts with beaten egg and bake for 10–12 minutes until risen and golden. Top each with a teaspoon of pesto and serve warm.

HAM RAREBIT WITH GHERKIN SALAD

MAKES 30

Preheat oven to 200°C / 400°F / gas 6. Slice a baguette as for Crostini on the previous page. Mix together 2 tablespoons olive oil, 3 tablespoons softened butter and 2 tablespoons wholegrain mustard. Brush over both sides of each baguette slice and bake for 8 minutes until crisp. Make gherkin salad by mixing 10 finely chopped cocktail gherkins, 2 finely chopped shallots and 1 tablespoon olive oil. Preheat a hot grill. Top each toast with a piece of thinly sliced ham (85 g / 3 oz in total), then a wafer-thin shaving of Cheddar (100 g / 4 oz in total). Season and grill until cheese melts. Top with a spoonful of gherkin salad to serve.

SCALLOPS AND SAGE WRAPPED IN BACON

MAKES 20

Preheat oven to 200°C / 400°F / gas 6. Place a sage leaf on top of each of 20 medium scallops (or 10 large, cut horizontally into 2 rounds). Stretch 20 rashers of smoked streaky bacon with the back of a knife, then cut each in half lengthwise. Wrap a bacon strip around each scallop and then wrap another around, across the first to enclose scallop completely. Brush with some garlic-infused oil (see the Duck with Kumquat recipe, left) and bake for 10–12 minutes until crisp. Serve speared with cocktail sticks.

Vegetable Skewers

PREPARATION: ABOUT 30 MINUTES
COOKING: ABOUT 30 MINUTES
MAKES 25

2 red peppers, cored and deseeded but left whole
1 butternut squash, peeled, halved, seeded and cut lengthwise into 1 cm / 1/2 inch slices
8 tbsp olive oil
2 garlic cloves, crushed
1 tsp each ground coriander and paprika
salt and pepper
1 aubergine, sliced lengthwise
140 g / 5 oz soft goats' cheese
2 tsp toasted cumin seeds
25 woody rosemary sprigs (optional)

1 Preheat oven to 220°C / 425°F / gas 7. Put peppers and squash slices on a baking sheet. In a bowl, mix the oil, garlic, coriander, paprika and seasoning. Brush over the squash. Bake for 15 minutes.
2 Transfer squash to a plate. Put peppers in a plastic bag, seal and allow to cool.
3 Put the aubergine slices on a baking sheet, brush with some oil mixture and bake for 10 minutes; set aside to cool.
4 Spread the cheese all over half the aubergine slices and sprinkle with cumin. Sandwich with remaining aubergine slices. Cut sandwiches and squash into 25 × 3 cm / 10 × 1 1/4 inch squares.
5 Peel skins off peppers and cut flesh into 25 × 3 cm / 10 × 1 1/4 inch squares.
6 Layer the vegetables, alternating the colours, then spear with a rosemary sprig or cocktail stick and place on a baking sheet. Brush with the remaining oil mixture and bake for 3–5 minutes to heat through. Serve warm.

Mini Roast Potatoes

Small or baby potatoes are ideal for roasting and topping; served warm as canapés, they're so tasty. Look out for packs of small Charlotte potatoes in the supermarket.

PREPARATION: 30 MINUTES
COOKING: 30–40 MINUTES
MAKES 16 PIECES

WHAT YOU DO

Preheat the oven to 190°C / 375°F / gas 5. Toss 8 small potatoes in 2 tablespoons of olive oil and tip into a roasting tin. Sprinkle with coarse sea salt and freshly ground black pepper, then roast for 30–40 minutes until tender. Leave the potatoes to stand until they are cool enough to handle, then split them in half lengthwise.

MAKE AHEAD

Cook the potatoes up to 2 hours ahead, but don't cut them in half. Let them cool completely, then cover and store in the fridge. Warm through before serving, or serve at room temperature.

THE TOPPINGS:
INSTANT CORONATION CHICKEN

Put 25 g / 1 oz roughly chopped cooked chicken in a bowl with 1 tablespoon of chopped, deseeded red pepper. Stir in 1 tablespoon of fromage frais, 1 teaspoon of curry paste, 2 teaspoons of mango chutney and 1 tablespoon of chopped fresh parsley. Carefully spoon on to 4 potato halves, cover and chill until needed.

BLUE CHEESE AND CHIVES

Crumble 25 g / 1 oz blue cheese and divide between 4 potato halves. Sprinkle over 1 tablespoon of chopped fresh chives. Just before serving, grill for 1–2 minutes until the cheese is bubbling.

SMOKED SALMON
AND HORSERADISH

Mix 1 teaspoon of horseradish sauce with 1 tablespoon of crème fraîche and divide between 4 potato halves. Tear 25 g / 1 oz smoked salmon into 8 pieces and put 2 on top of each potato half. Cover and chill until needed.

CRÈME FRAÎCHE
AND SPRING ONION

Season 2 tablespoons of crème fraîche with salt and pepper, then divide between 4 potato halves. Chop 2 spring onions and sprinkle over the potatoes. Cover and chill. Just before serving, sprinkle with a little freshly ground black pepper.

Acknowledgments

Recipes by

Sue Ashworth
New vegetables à la grecque p26, Three-bean salad with citrus dressing p54, Roasted vegetable quiche p69

Lindsey Bareham
Feta and herb briouats p29, Potatoes sautéed with garlic and onion p124

Annie Bell
Warm salad of roasted aubergine, tomatoes and cannellini beans p34

Angela Boggiano
Simple curried vegetable broth p13, Grilled sweet potato and beetroot salad p49, Shallot tatin p75, Vegetable lasagne p83, Roast filled onions p88, Basic baked potato p116, Blue cheese and herb jackets p116, Spinach, mushroom and egg jackets p116, Hummus and avocado salsa jackets p116, Aubergine chilli jackets p116, Spiced roast potatoes p119, Roast potatoes p120, Red onion, garlic and rosemary roasties p121, Hasselback potatoes p122, Pan haggerty p127, Potato rösti p128, Soufflé potatoes p130, Chips p131, Basic mashed potato p132, Aligot p132, Leek and mustard mash p132, Herb and Parmesan mash p132, Colcannon p132, Clapshot p132, Champ p132, Hummus falafel p149

Lorna Brash
Caldo verde p10, Honeyed carrot and fig couscous p32, Tricolor muffins p44, Tarragon mushrooms with bean mash p47, Summer vegetable lattice pie p69, Polenta squash layer p81, Grilled vegetable pasticcio p98, Marinated couscous with harissa tomatoes p99, Pakoras with spicy yoghurt dip p148

Mary Cadogan
Spicy gazpacho with basil p10, Mozzarella pasta with olives and chilli p100, Leek and blue cheese risotto p104

Robert Carrier
Tomato stacks with herb and onion salsa p31, Thai spring rolls with chilli dipping sauce p142

Gilly Cubitt
Stoved new potatoes and mushrooms p127, Vegetable stir-fry with filo noodles p139

Lewis Esson
Vegetable stock p17, Green vegetable curry with shiitake mushrooms p143

Joanna Farrow
Mushroom wonton soup p14, Warm maple-glazed vegetable salad with feta and walnuts p50

Ursula Ferrigno
Fennel raviolini pp94-5, Fennel raviolini with roasted vegetable and saffron sauce p97

Rebecca Ford
Chinese broth with curly kale seaweed p12, Asparagus with lime and coriander butter p36, Potato cakes with Swiss chard and hollandaise p44, Tomato and oregano pizza p113, Pimiento, rocket and mozzarella pizza p113

Silvana Franco
Creamy mushroom lasagne p82, Cheesy spaghetti with courgettes and bacon p92, Spicy pepper penne p98

Paul Gayler
Chestnut gnocchi with sour cranberries p107, Potato latkes with herb-grilled feta p128

Susanna Gelmetti
Fennel risotto p104, Pizza from scratch pp108-9, Pizza toppings pp110-1

The Good Food Team
Chickpea and tomato broth p23, Feta and anchovy stuffed peppers p26, Aubergine and mozzarella stacks p30, Vegetable omelette p35, Asparagus and soft egg tartlets p38, Roasted asparagus with poached eggs p38, Roast ham and mushroom toast p40,

Garlicky mushroom toasts p43, Butter bean, olive and feta salad p61, Caesar salad with Parmesan crisps p62, Goats' cheese and onion tarts p72, Leek, ham and Camembert grill p79, Pasta with broccoli and toasted nuts p92, Tomato and mushroom stacks p100, Oven egg and chips p119

Clare Gordon-Smith
Vegetable patties with spicy tomato chutney p31, from her book, *Flavouring with Chillies* (Ryland, Peters & Small). Reprinted by permission of the Peters Fraser and Dunlop Group Limited on behalf of the author.

Peter Gorton
Spiced lentil soup with lemon yoghurt p13, Baked goats' cheese parcels with sweet-and-sour leeks p27, from his restaurant, The Horn of Plenty, Devon

Mark Gregory
Udon noodles with miso and roast ginger pumpkin p136, from his restaurant t'su, London

Jane Grigson
Jane Grigson's spicy parsnip soup p16, from her book, *Jane Grigson's Vegetable Book* (Penguin Books)

Sophie Grigson
Roast squash with lime and caper sauce p88, Spaghetti alla puttanesca p93

Alastair Hendy
Roast vine tomatoes and onions with cheddar p40, Field mushrooms with truffle oil on Italian country toast p40, Spicy avocado on coriander cornbread toast p40, Garlic sesame dip with crispy pittas p148, Mushroom frittata p151, Mini crab tortilla p151, Pâté crostini with onion marmalade p151, Smoked salmon and horseradish crostini p151, Mozzarella with Mediterranean tomato salsa p151, Duck with kumquat and shallot relish p152, Tomato tartlets with pesto p152, Ham rarebit with gherkin salad p152, Scallops and sage

wrapped in bacon p152, Vegetable skewers p152

Ken Hom
Vegetable salad with curry-soy vinaigrette p54, from his book, *Travels with a Hot Wok* (BBC Books)

Sybil Kapoor
Hoisin Chinese noodles p138

Orlando Murrin
Jerusalem artichoke soup p22, Sausage-stuffed cabbage p84, Roman spinach p102

Angela Nilsen
Old-fashioned tomato sauce p20, Cherry tomato and basil clafoutis p47, Salad dressings pp56-7, French onion tart p73, Tomato tarte tatin p75, Chilli oil p140

Meena Pathak
Spicy green lentils with crispy onions p143, Cabbage paratha with sesame seeds p144, Cauliflower, beans and tomatoes with mustard seeds p144

Gary Rhodes
Warm poached eggs on potato salad p49, Asparagus, sea kale and red onion salad with spicy potato croutons and soured cream and chive dressing p61, Macaroni cheese pie with artichokes and mushroom p66, Provençale tarts with pesto sauce p70

Lyn Rutherford
Mediterranean salad p62

Bridget Sargeson
Velvety cauliflower cheese soup p19, Minty pea and ham soup p19

Vanessa Scott
Goats' cheese and olive toasts p43

Bill Sewell
Leek and potato Hereford pie p67, from his restaurants The Place Below, London, and Café@All Saints, Hereford

Mary Spyrou
Hummus p149

Carla Tomasi
Piedmontese peppers p50

Linda Tubby
Goats' cheese polenta with mushrooms p32, Scalloped potato and rich cheese flan p122, Brussels sprout satay p142

The Vegetarian Good Food Team
Chilled beetroot soup with horseradish cream p22, Carrot and potato flat bread p79

Becca Watson
Fiorelli with oven-dried vegetables and tapenade p97, from her book, *Perfect Pasta* (Merehurst Ltd)

Jenny White
Salted runner beans p52, Spinach and Gruyère tart p73, Jerusalem artichoke and mushroom dauphinoise p76, Polenta, red pepper and courgette gratin p80, Cabbage parcels with roasted ratatouille p86, Mini roast potatoes p154

Antony Worrall Thompson
Dandelion leaves with pear, Roquefort and hazelnuts p58

Peter Wright
Puy lentil salad p59, Tamari toasted seed coleslaw p59, Tian of courgettes p81

Photographers

William Adams-Lingwood
Piedmontese peppers p50

Marie-Louise Avery
Roast squash with lime and caper sauce p89, Spaghetti alla puttanesca p93, Roast potatoes step-by-steps pp120-1, Hummus p149

Martin Brigdale
Mushroom wonton soup pp14-5, Warm maple-glazed vegetable salad

with feta and walnuts p51, Salad dressing step-by-steps p56, Salad p57, Roasted vegetable quiche p68

Robin Broadbent
Provençale tarts with pesto sauce p71

Peter Cassidy
Chestnut gnocchi with sour cranberries p106, Udon noodles with miso and roast ginger pumpkin p137

Jean Cazals
Old-fashioned tomato sauce p20, Tomatoes p21, Cherry tomato and basil clafoutis p46, Salted runner beans p52, Runner beans p53, Tomato tarte tatin p74, Mozzarella pasta with olives and chilli p101, Fennel risotto p104, Pizza toppings pp110-1, Chillies p140, Chilli oil p141

Mick Dean
Jane Grigson's spicy parsnip soup step-by-steps pp16-7

Ken Field
Tricolor muffins p45, Hoisin Chinese noodles p138

Gus Filgate
Leek and potato Hereford pie p67

David Jordan
Caldo verde p11, Puy lentil salad p59

Dave King
Baked goats' cheese parcels with sweet-and-sour leeks p27

Graham Kirk
Velvety cauliflower cheese soup p18

Jess Koppel
Grilled sweet potato and beetroot salad p49, Roast filled onions p88

Sandra Lane
Brussels sprout satay p142

David Munns
Sausage-stuffed cabbage p84, Cabbage p85, Roman spinach p102, Spinach p103

James Murphy
Asparagus and soft egg tartlets p38

Thomas Odulate
Fennel raviolini step-by-steps pp94-5, Fennel raviolini with roasted vegetable and saffron sauce p96, Potato latkes with herb-grilled feta p129

William Reavell
Chinese broth with curly kale seaweed p12, Potato cakes with Swiss chard and hollandaise p44, Stoved new potatoes and mushrooms p127, Vegetable stir-fry with filo noodles p139

Roger Stowell
Spicy gazpacho with basil p8, Jerusalem artichoke soup p22, Chickpea and tomato broth p23, Roasted vegetable omelette p35, Spicy avocado on coriander cornbread toast p40, Roast ham and mushroom roast p40, Field mushrooms with truffle oil on Italian country toast p40, Roast vine tomatoes and onions with cheddar p41, Warm poached eggs on potato salad p48, Butter bean, olive and feta salad p61, Caesar salad with Parmesan crisps p63, Macaroni cheese pie with artichokes and mushroom p64, Leek, ham and Camembert grill p78, Polenta, red pepper and courgette gratin p80, Pasta with broccoli and toasted nuts p90, Basic baked potato p114, Blue cheese and herb jackets p116, Spinach, mushroom and egg jackets p116, Aubergine chilli jackets p116, Hummus and avocado salsa jackets p117, Oven egg and chips p118, Spiced roast potatoes p119, Red onion, garlic and rosemary roasties p121, Hasselback potatoes p122, Pan haggerty p126, Potato rösti p128, Soufflé potatoes p130, Chips p131, Aligot p132, Leek and mustard mash p132, Herb and Parmesan mash p132, Basic mashed potato p133, Spring vegetable noodles p134, Cauliflower, beans and tomatoes with mustard seeds p145, Garlic sesame dip with crispy pittas p146, Canapés pp150-1, Grilled vegetable and goats' cheese skewers p153

Sam Stowell
Dandelion leaves with pear, Roquefort and hazelnuts p58, Jerusalem artichoke and mushroom dauphinoise p76, Artichokes p77

Martin Thompson
Creamy mushroom lasagne p82

Trevor Vaughan
Marinated couscous with harissa tomatoes p99

Philip Webb
Feta and Piedmontese peppers p24, Feta and herb briouats p28, Feta and herb briouats (detail) p29, Aubergine and mozzarella stacks p30, Aubergine and mozzarella stacks (detail) p30, Goats' cheese polenta with mushrooms p33, Warm salad of roasted aubergine, tomatoes and cannellini beans p34, Asparagus p37, Roasted asparagus with poached eggs p39, Garlicky mushroom toasts p42, Three-bean salad with citrus dressing p55, Goats' cheese and onion tarts p72, Goats' cheese and onion tarts step-by-step p72, Cabbage parcels with roasted ratatouille p86, Scalloped potato and rich cheese flan p123, Potatoes sautéed with garlic and onion p124, Potatoes p125, Mini roast potatoes pp154-5

Simon Wheeler
Leek and blue cheese risotto p105

Frank Wieder
Asparagus with lime and coriander butter p36, Summer vegetable lattice pie p69, Tomato and oregano pizza p112

Geoff Wilkinson
Pizza base step-by-steps pp108-9

Whilst every effort has been made to trace and acknowledge all copyright holders, we would like to apologize should there be any errors or omissions.

Index